SCARS OF *grace*

GRACE. We can all agree that we throw around this "churchy" word from time to time. And yet, when we truly think about it, we realize that we don't really understand the fullness of that word. We aren't aware of the bold promise that grace holds or comprehend the power of healing that lies in those five letters.

We tend to limit the impact of grace in our lives because we only associate grace with what Jesus did on the cross. We understand that Jesus paid for our sins: past, present and future; but that is just the beginning of the truth about grace.

Even with the awareness of Jesus' sacrifice, do you still feel the burden of sin and brokenness within you? Do you still walk around everyday and feel the guilt, shame and condemnation of your sins weighing you down? Or do you simply wonder, "How can grace transform my life?

Take 12 weeks with us to unpack the vast meaning of scars of grace and explore what that means in your life. In addition to solid biblical teaching, we will hear the raw and personal stories of relatable women and how grace transformed young women's lives. Daily devotional journals will take us deeper into scripture and provide a place for us to connect with Jesus and allow Him to turn our deepest wounds into beautiful scars of His grace.

SCARS
OF *grace*

LAURA DUDEK

Table of Contents

Weekly Reflection

Take a few moments to quiet yourself before the Lord. Find your comfy spot, or retreat to a place where you often meet with the Lord. In that place, allow your heart, mind and soul to rest into the presence of God. Turn off the distractions, put your to-do list away, and simply be in the present moment. This is your time to be transparent with the Lord, to lay before him your wounds, hurts and struggles, and lift up your requests and deepest desires. You may praise Him, sit in the stillness and listen, or cry to release pain or hurt. The only thing you need to be is real with your heavenly Papa. You may pray the prayer below, or dive into your own. May this time be a blessing to your heart; may the Lord speak to you in new ways; may you allow the comforting and healing hands of our Father reach out to you; and may you allow the peace and joy of the Holy Spirit to pour over you.

Lord Jesus,

I am expecting to hear your voice in this moment. Open my heart and my mind to experience and hear your truth in a new way. I lay my wounds and brokenness before you, in hope and anticipation that you will heal it all. May I hear new revelation this week! May I see you and your truth in a new light! Wrap your grace around me and speak softly to your daughter. I am here to listen.

Amen.

Dear Jesus,

(Gods intention in creation)

(Prayer for this study)

The Fall

> "So the LORD God banished him from the Garden of Eden to work
> the ground from which he had been taken. After he drove them out,
> he placed on the east side of the Garden of Eden cherubim and a flaming
> sword flashing back and forth to guard the way to the tree of life."
>
> ### Genesis 3:23-24

God created the universe in complete perfection. Every living thing lived in harmony. God Himself was present in the midst of his creation and even walked alongside Adam and Eve in the garden of Eden.

But then came harmony's destruction. A single distortion, a single lie, a single question from Satan- and it was all shattered. Adam and Eve chose to believe the craftiness of Satan above the command of God. That one moment in time, that one decision by two humans, that one choice to believe a serpent instead of their creator impacted the world and humanity for all time.

The consequences of that sin are heartbreaking. Adam and Eve were tossed out of the garden, cast away, never to return to its splendor and goodness. We read about the curses for both men and women in chapter 3:16-19. It was because of that single act of disobedience that life from that moment on would be strenuous and laborious for humanity.

Even more devastating than those curses, was the relational shift between God and humanity. No longer would God walk side by side His people. No longer could they be in His very presence. With sin standing between God and His sons and daughters, humanity no longer could enjoy the blissful, peaceful and holy presence of their Father. Sin tainted humanity and made us unfit to be in the midst of a perfect God.

Since that moment, God has been on mission to restore His people back to Himself. He planned and set about a way to bring His creation back into a redeemed relationship so that He could walk alongside us again.

Imagine walking side by side with God. What would that scene look like? Can you imagine the experience of being cast out of God's presence? What emotions would be evoked in that scenario?

_____

_____

_____

_____

_____

_____

_____

_____

_____

_____

_____

_____

_____

_____

_____

_____

_____

_____

_____

The Law

> "When the Lord finished speaking to Moses on Mount Sinai,
> he gave him the two tablets of the covenant law,
> the tablets of stone inscribed by the finger of God."
>
> **Exodus 31:18**

When many people think about "the law," they tend to think about it as this overbearing and burdensome yoke that was looming over the nation of Israel. We seem to associate the law with condemnation, guilt and most of all, legalism. But that is only one side of the coin. We must understand that the law in the Old Testament was God's way of allowing Israel to be in relationship with Him. It was His loving way of providing a system that would enable His people to receive blessing and favor from Him.

The entire book of Leviticus was filled with crystal clear commands that God expected the Israelites to fulfill. This system was entirely conditional; God would only bless the Israelites when they fulfilled each and every condition perfectly.

One of the foundational aspects of the law was sacrifice. God was extremely specific about this element because it was through sacrifice that people could temporarily be washed clean from their sin. The only way in which they could become presentable to God would be through the shedding of specific animals' innocent blood. Therefore, the animal that was offered had to be absolutely perfect, without any blemish or defect. This ceremony of sacrifice represented the image of the sinner placing their guilt upon that animal and the animal's purity and innocence being imparted on the sinner.

This transfer of innocence and sin was the only way which people could be made clean and in right relational standing with God. However this system was flawed. God never meant it to be the "end all, be all" solution. It was merely a temporary fix. The permanent solution was on its way, but for the time being, the law was God's loving and brief resolution.

When you think about "The Law," what comes to mind? How do you feel that the "law-like," legalistic mentality has affected you?

_____

_____

_____

_____

_____

_____

_____

_____

_____

_____

_____

_____

_____

_____

_____

_____

_____

_____

The Favor Equation

"Moses bowed to the ground at once and worshiped. 'Lord,' he said,
'if I have found favor in your eyes, then let the Lord go with us. Although
this is a stiff-necked people, forgive our wickedness and
our sin, and take us as your inheritance."

Exodus 34:8-9

God formed a covenant with the nation of Israel. In this covenant, the nation was called to live in obedience to the law and was expected to uphold every command to the last letter. At first glance, we don't see grace in this form of interaction. In our view, we simply see each of the 613 commands as a tool to point out people's behavior so that they could be utterly aware of their sins. But that is only half of the truth. Yes, the purpose of the law was to make the people aware of their sin, because anytime a standard is set for an individual, he or she immediately compares him or herself to that standard to see where they fall. But, the greater purpose of the law was to give the Israelites the opportunity to receive the grace of God. In the Old Testament, the concept of "grace" was much more closely connected to the idea of "favor." Therefore, when we search for the word "grace" in the Old Testament, we will often find the translated word "favor" in its place.

In this flawed system of relationship, the favor of God was contingent upon the obedience of the people. If they did not obey God's command, then God's favor (victory in battle, His provision of food, His protection against enemies) could not be ensured. The favor, or grace, of God was reduced to a simple transaction: the people do this and God gives them that. It was only in the moments when God's people were living in complete and total obedience to His laws that He could bless them the way he desired. This mode of blessing was God's temporary means of providing his presence, protection and provision to His people who were marked with sin and separated from His pure and supreme companionship.

Have you ever thought about grace in terms of this transaction? How does this scenario feel to you? In your opinion, what does God's favor look like?

_____

_____

_____

_____

_____

_____

_____

_____

_____

_____

_____

_____

_____

_____

_____

_____

_____

_____

_____

_____

Holy, Holy, Holy

> "And they were calling to one another: 'Holy, holy, holy is the Lord Almighty; the whole earth is full of his glory.' At the sound of their voices the doorposts and thresholds shook and the temple was filled with smoke. 'Woe to me!' I cried. 'I am ruined! For I am a man of unclean lips, and I live among a people of unclean lips, and my eyes have seen the King, the Lord Almighty.'"
>
> **Isaiah 6:3-5**

It is here in these verses we read about Isaiah's commission to be a prophet of the Lord. These verses paint a beautiful picture of God's infinite holiness. We know that the gift of grace through Jesus is the one thing that now allows us to be in the presence of God. So as we begin to uncover the deeper meaning and power of grace, we must first understand the immense holiness of God. We need to have a clear awareness of how far we fall from that divine level of holiness.

The word *holy* has an intense meaning; it defines something as being set apart from other people or things. It defines an object or being as distinct and sacred. Isaiah describes the seraphim, a group of angels, singing about the Lord, "Holy, holy, holy." This repetition three times isn't just for an extra "oomph" to make the song better; there is a purpose in those three words. In the Hebrew language, repetition equaled a greater intensity of meaning. Therefore saying God was "holy" was a significant deal. Saying God was "Holy, holy" was saying that He was "really, really, really" holy. But then to say that God was "Holy, holy, holy" meant that He is the highest form of holy; He is set apart, distinct and sacred to a degree that we cannot even fathom in our human rationale.

Therefore when we think of grace, we have to see it through the lens of God's consuming and vast holiness. We are interacting, having relationship, with the creator of the entire universe; the One who gives life, the One who literally spoke and created the earth. This is a huge deal. The gap that needed to be bridged between fallen humanity and perfect God was not a mere hop away. It was a bridge that only God Himself could form, and no amount of human effort could ever travel that distance.

Have you ever thought about God's consuming and extreme Holiness? Imagine yourself as Isaiah—how would you respond if you entered into this scene?

_____

_____

_____

_____

_____

_____

_____

_____

_____

_____

_____

_____

_____

_____

_____

_____

_____

_____

_____

Consequences

> "For the wages of sin is death, but the gift of God is eternal life in Christ Jesus our Lord."
>
> **Romans 6:23**

D eath. That's what humanity deserves for its sin. We consistently rebel against the Lord. We worship other Gods. We disobey God's commands. But sin didn't enter the world alone; along with it came brokenness, decay, destruction, and most tragic of all- death.

The thing is, God never desired to bring these terrible things into the world. We don't see a part in Genesis when God said, "Let there be destruction," and then "He saw that it was good." We don't see that in the creation story because it wasn't something that God created. Many people think that the world is filled with destruction, pain, tragic events and horrible disasters because God spoke those things into existence. They mistakenly extend the creation story to say that after God created a beautiful world, He then sent it into complete chaos and ruin.

But remember back to the very first day of this study. In the third chapter of the entire Bible we saw that a *man* and *woman* disobeyed God. We read that because of that act of disobedience they were cast away from God. Therefore, the fault is on humanity's shoulders- we were the ones who brought sin into this world. And with that sin came curses, affliction, suffering, and death.

Even in our choice to walk away from God, He still pursued his creation. He never gave up hope on those who bore his very image. He never stopped loving the very beings that brought him the greatest joy.

Think about the despair you would feel if there was only death coming to you. Only hardship with no blessing. Only pain and suffering with no payoff. Only brokenness but no healing. Only death and no resurrection.

Have you ever found yourself believing that God intended to create destruction and pain? How does it change your view of God to know that he didn't actually desire for there to be brokenness and hardship in the world?

_____

_____

_____

_____

_____

_____

_____

_____

_____

_____

_____

_____

_____

_____

_____

_____

_____

_____

_____

When God found me, I was lonely and committing many sins that I didn't realize were even sins at the time. I was still healing from a bad break up a few months prior and I was heading into a two week long vacation. Though my relationship with my Dad was strained, he offered to let me ride with him in his truck (he is a truck driver) across the country. I only had seen my dad one to two times a year and we barely spoke on the phone, but I thought this was as good a time as any to spend some time with him. That was the summer of 2009. Although I didn't know it at the time, God was working on saving me. During that trip, my dad took me to his home church, which was a tiny church, in what I thought was the middle of nowhere, in North Carolina. I had grown up Presbyterian, but had rebelled against going to church during my teen years and hadn't been since. What I found was a pastor who spoke from the heart and it felt like he was preaching right to me!

I had never experienced anything like it. During that trip, I got to know my father a little better as well as God. When I returned to New York, I went back to living my life, but God kept popping up everywhere.

He wasn't going to give up on me. I decided to ask coworkers about churches they were going to and decided to join one of them at their church in October 2009. That day was the day I gave my life to Christ. I can't say that I was good at living like a Christian because I had a hard time letting go of my old life. I felt like I was missing out on the worldly things so I continued to drink and partake in the wrong kinds of relationships. God never gave up on me and showed me so much mercy. He continued to work on my heart and slowly I began to listen to Him. In a few short months, I no longer felt the need to drink or be in relationships that I knew were not healthy. What I was truly missing out on was allowing God to help me lead my life and having a true relationship with Him. A year later, in January of 2011, I publicly dedicated my life to Jesus Christ by getting baptized. I have been in relationship with Him every day since and I can't picture a life without Him in it!

Amanda

Weekly Reflection

Take a few moments to quiet yourself before the Lord. Find your comfy spot, or retreat to a place where you often meet with the Lord. In that place, allow your heart, mind and soul to rest into the presence of God. Turn off the distractions, put your to-do list away, and simply be in the present moment. This is your time to be transparent with the Lord, to lay before him your wounds, hurts and struggles, and lift up your requests and deepest desires. You may praise Him, sit in the stillness and listen, or cry to release pain or hurt. The only thing you need to be is real with your heavenly Papa. You may pray the prayer below, or dive into your own. May this time be a blessing to your heart; may the Lord speak to you in new ways; may you allow the comforting and healing hands of our Father reach out to you; and may you allow the peace and joy of the Holy Spirit to pour over you.

Lord Jesus,

I am expecting to hear your voice in this moment. Open my heart and my mind to experience and hear your truth in a new way. I lay my wounds and brokenness before you, in hope and anticipation that you will heal it all. May I hear new revelation this week! May I see you and your truth in a new light! Wrap your grace around me and speak softly to your daughter. I am here to listen.

Amen.

Dear Jesus,

Flawed

> "...the law brings wrath. And where there is no law,
> there is no transgression."
>
> **Romans 4:15**

The law was a blessing to the Israelites for many reasons. However, it also held God's people to a higher standard, a holy standard. And so with the presence of the law, came the ability to break the law. In the same hands meant for people to receive God's presence once again, was also the opportunity for them to commit trespasses against that same God.

Romans 3:20 sums up this idea perfectly, "Therefore no one will be declared righteous in God's sight by observing the law; rather, through the law we become conscious of our sin." The purpose of the law was not to perfect people, but to show them their complete inadequacy before the God that created them. It was a filter through which God spoke to His creation to show them that He alone is perfect and holy. They were called to imitate who He is. He is holy, therefore they are holy.

With the factors of a perfect law and imperfect people, sin's presence in the world was inevitable. People could not live up to this standard on their own. A flawed people could not fulfill a flawless law. The law then, through our inability to fulfill it, would ultimately bring punishment upon us.

This concept seems unfair. Why in the world would God make people strive to live up to a standard that only God Himself can live up to? Why would He punish people, even put some to death, because they couldn't reach a standard that was humanly unreachable? God was setting up the perfect circumstances through which He could display his vast greatness and give Himself the highest glory.

Have you ever felt like you couldn't be good enough to make God happy? Have you ever wrestled with trying to be perfect for God? What did that battle look like? If you haven't wrestled with that, what truth has given you a firm foundation of freedom from this battle?

_____

_____

_____

_____

_____

_____

_____

_____

_____

_____

_____

_____

_____

_____

_____

_____

_____

_____

The Great Divide

"For all have sinned and fall short of the glory of God,
and all are justified freely by his grace through the redemption
that came by Christ Jesus."

Romans 3:23-24

For a long time in my own life I thought I was "deserving" of God's grace because I had never done anything "wrong." Up until college I had never sworn, drunk, gone "too far" with a guy or severely disobeyed my parents. I had avoided all of the "big" sins and so in my mind I was "worthy" of God's love. But I didn't realize that my very nature was steeped in sin. My gossiping tongue, my jealousy for what other's had, my little white lies, my silent voice not telling my friends about Jesus- the list could go on of all the things that I never even considered that counted me out of God's presence.

I never made a clear conscious choice to do those things, but I never had to in order to be a sinner. It was purely my very nature that led me to do them. My jealous nature made me want what others had. My pride led me to lie to protect myself. My desire for approval led me to talk about others to get them on my side. So I learned that even while I never chose to be a sinner, I was still indeed one to my very core.

We can all have moments when we think that we are "good enough" to receive God's grace. And if we aren't "good enough," we certainly aren't as bad as "those" people. We constantly play this game of wondering where we stand in the sin scale. We think if we aren't "that bad" then we pass the test and we become worthy of being in God's presence.

But what I had to realize was that even those "petty" sins cast me out of God's presence. Even those tiny blemishes on my record deemed me unworthy to meet face to face with my holy and perfect God. What I thought were insignificant sins created the most gigantic divide between me and my Creator.

Have you ever found yourself in this situation? Have you ever thought you were "just good enough" (or possibly that you weren't "that bad"), and therefore, pass the test?

_____

_____

_____

_____

_____

_____

_____

_____

_____

_____

_____

_____

_____

_____

_____

_____

_____

_____

_____

_____

_____

Aftermath

"As for you, you were dead in your transgressions and sins, in which you used to live when you followed the ways of this world and of the ruler of the kingdom of the air, the spirit who is now at work in those who are disobedient. All of us also lived among them at one time, gratifying the cravings of our flesh and following its desires and thoughts. Like the rest, we were by nature deserving of wrath."

Ephesians 2:1-3

We still feel the effects of the fall today. We see the aftermath of Adam and Eve's decision in this world: brokenness, pain, murder, theft, rape, curses, etc. We see the nature of a fallen world around us, just turn on the news and you'll see countless examples of this.

We don't just see the affects around us, but inside of us too. We see the casualties within our own soul inflicted by sin. We can feel how sin changed us, molded us, cursed us, broke us, marred us, and wounded us. We can see our jaded hearts, our own unhealthiness and our own sin that has made us something that we never thought we would ever be. And when we see all of that, we feel stuck in our muck.

There have been times when I feel the weight of my brokenness as if a concrete truck just dumped on me. And then the concrete dries, and I'm permanently stuck in it. Sometimes, I have felt dead in my sin, completely lifeless because of my shame and guilt. I have felt paralyzed by my shortcomings, so conscious of how fallen I am. I have experienced moments where I am acutely aware of my own jagged edges, my ungodly behavior, and the pain that is caused by all of that mess.

I'm not sure about you, but there have been times when I feel hopeless in the hold that my chains have on me. I see the fallen world around me, and even greater, I see the fallenness in me. It simultaneously makes me angry and depressed; angry at my inability to fix anything and depressed that I am permanently cemented in all my junk.

But Paul says here, "You were once dead," more accurately read, "You were *once* dead." We are no longer dead or cemented in our wounds or stuck in our brokenness. There is now a way out.

What does your "cement" look like? What brokenness do you feel is looming over you and pinning you down?

_____

_____

_____

_____

_____

_____

_____

_____

_____

_____

_____

_____

_____

_____

_____

_____

_____

_____

_____

_____

Overflow

> "Now Cain said to his brother Abel, 'Let's go out to the field.' While they were in the field, Cain attacked his brother Abel and killed him."
>
> **Genesis 4:8**

Read the full story of Cain and Abel in Genesis 4:1-16. There is a reason why the next recorded sin after Adam and Eve is about their sons. God is showing us the full picture of sin. Sin doesn't just cause shame and guilt internally, but it also affects us relationally.

Sin mars our relationships- our marriages, our friendships, our family, our interactions with strangers, our communication with professors or coworkers. We see this very situation in the fourth chapter of the entire Bible! Jealousy overwhelmed Cain, depicting his and our sinful nature in action. That jealousy poured out of Cain and his reaction was to sin against his brother, so he literally murdered him!

Today we see relational sin all over the place. We have all had someone else's brokenness affect us. Whether our wounds were just a scratch or a deep, life-threatening gash, we have all felt the sting of sin in our relationships. We experience how our best friend betrayed us. We see our family gossip about each other. We watch as marriages fall apart, babies are abandoned to be raised by a single mother, uncles raping their nieces, co-workers attempting to sabotage us, and the list goes on.

It's a disgusting picture, isn't it? But it is all the effect of a sin tarnished world. We were not originally created to be hurtful, angry, selfish people, but then sin shattered our very nature and started seeping out of us and flowing onto others. At the very root of all evil, each painful moment, and every wound inflicted upon us, is the presence of a fallen, sin-filled, and broken heart.

Where have you seen/currently see relational sin in your life? Can you see the situation through a broken sin-tainted lens, meaning that you can are able to see into the individual's heart issues that stem from the fall?

_____

_____

_____

_____

_____

_____

_____

_____

_____

_____

_____

_____

_____

_____

_____

_____

_____

_____

The Right Time

> "You see, at just the right time, when we were still powerless, Christ
> died for the ungodly. Very rarely will anyone die for a righteous person,
> though for a good person someone might possibly dare to die.
> But God demonstrates his own love for us in this:
> While we were still sinners, Christ died for us."
>
> **Romans 5:6-8**

At just the right time Christ died for us. What did that time look like? Was it when humanity finally reached the standard of "good enough" to be saved? Did God send Jesus when He saw that we were getting the hang of the law, and so we could finally handle a Savior?

Paul says here that the right time, the moment when God decided to send His only Son, was the moment when we were absolutely dead in sin and powerless to do anything for ourselves. God knew that we were too weak to help *ourselves* out of sin. God saw His creation, His people, walking in disobedience to His commands, continually stiff-arming His word, and yet He felt compassion for His creation which was cemented in their sin and brokenness. This pivotal moment of change was an action of complete love and empathy for a creation damaged by trouble and affliction.

This point is so important for us to understand! This choice of timing shows us a fundamental truth of God. We were powerless, but God is all powerful. We were helpless to conquer sin, but God is the almighty victor. We were dead, but God is the author of resurrection.

The gap between the most holy being in the entire universe, and fallen, sinful humanity, is larger than we can imagine. No amount of trying- no matter how hard or how high- could ever bring us back to the restored relationship with our creator. There is not one person who can live up to the perfect law, not one. There is no one good enough, no one "holy" enough, no one strong enough to mend the sin scarred relationship between Creator and His Creation. Sin has cast us far, far off from our God. But in our colossal distance from God- at just the right time- when we were paralyzed to save ourselves, He threw us a life saver to draw us back in.

Have you ever let it sink in that God sent Jesus when we were absolutely helpless to do anything for ourselves? How does this truth make you feel? Are you overwhelmed with gratitude, or does it make you uncomfortable that you can't save yourself?

Grace Stories

As I think about my "Grace Story" I struggle a little because really there isn't just ONE story to tell. Looking back across my life, God has truly written His grace into countless moments of my life and is constantly and consistently drawing me closer into Himself.

It all started on a May evening over 20 years ago when my mother went into labor with her second child. While this was supposed to be a joyous occasion for our family, it was also filled with anxiety and fear; my mother was not due for almost three more months. As their child was born into this world only slightly more than 3lbs, the doctors confirmed my parents' fears: their child would not live. Trusting in the hope and new life found in Christ, my father and mother prayed over their new daughter in the hospital room only moments after her birth finding comfort in knowing that even if her earthly life was short, her life with God would be eternal. On that day, I, Rebekah Ruth, was not only born in an earthly sense, but also born again as I was welcomed into God's Family as his child through baptism. Obviously, since I'm writing this today, other miracles also occurred that day as God sustained my life when every doctor involved thought I wouldn't even live through the night.

God continued to pour out His grace in my life as I was raised in the home of two amazing Christian parents who loved the Lord with all their hearts and taught my sister and I to do the same. As wonderful as my childhood was, I slowly learned through the events of life that my father struggled with bipolar, depression, and anxiety disorders. Through medication and counseling, he was able to live a "normal" life throughout most of my childhood. However, in the spring of my 8th grade year, after resigning from his position as a Director of Christian Education at our church, the cycle of depression and anxiety became an everyday battle in our family. I cannot explain the pain and confusion in my middle and high school self when I saw a man who, not only had been a strong spiritual leader in my family but our entire church, not even able to attend church with us most Sundays. My father was around and tried to support and encourage our family, but for all practical purposes, most of the times he might as well have been a million miles away. It was in these moments that my Heavenly Father stepped in wrote even more grace into my story, drawing me into Himself and His great love.

This time in my life led me to place that seemed good and great on the outside, but slowly without even knowing, I was dying inside. I couldn't control what was happening to my dad, but I could control myself. I could get good grades and be the responsible "good girl" that didn't cause the family any more problems than we already had. I couldn't help him, but I could help others, and I did.

As I continued into college, there too, I saw God's grace. While there are parts of it I wouldn't trade for the world, and saw amazing ways in which God used my experience living with someone with a mental illness to help others in college struggling with similar issues, I eventually found myself in a place of codependency. Instead of finding my identity and wholeness in Christ, I began to find it in being able to help others. I needed to be needed and it was not a helpful, nor healthy, place to be anymore.

At the end of my four years of coursework I was sent by my school to New York for a yearlong internship at a Lutheran Church to finish my degree and certification. It was during that year, that God began to break down the walls that I had started building all the way back in 8th grade, walls that were helpful at the time, but had served their purpose and needed to come down. In my mind, I knew that there was nothing I could *do* to earn God's salvation, it was already done and paid for by Jesus, but my actions showed otherwise. As the walls slowly came down, God's grace began to reign in my heart. For the first time in a long time, my *heart* actually believed that God loved me. He loved me simply because I'm His child, not because of anything I did or didn't do. As God's grace rushed in to a heart I didn't even know was hurting, there was suddenly a joy and freedom I can't even begin to describe. Now I can serve God purely out of desire to know Him more and be close to Him, not out of duty or control or avoiding my own issues in life. As I'm in a healthier place I am even more able to truly help those around me.

God continues to write my grace story each and every day. As I struggle with the temptations of this world, as I long to know Him more, as I succeed and as I fail, as I seek to lead others to the freedom I've found; in it all, there is one constant: God's grace. And for that I couldn't be more thankful!

Rebekah

Weekly Reflection

Take a few moments to quiet yourself before the Lord. Find your comfy spot, or retreat to a place where you often meet with the Lord. In that place, allow your heart, mind and soul to rest into the presence of God. Turn off the distractions, put your to-do list away, and simply be in the present moment. This is your time to be transparent with the Lord, to lay before him your wounds, hurts and struggles, and lift up your requests and deepest desires. You may praise Him, sit in the stillness and listen, or cry to release pain or hurt. The only thing you need to be is real with your heavenly Papa. You may pray the prayer below, or dive into your own. May this time be a blessing to your heart; may the Lord speak to you in new ways; may you allow the comforting and healing hands of our Father reach out to you; and may you allow the peace and joy of the Holy Spirit to pour over you.

Lord Jesus,

I am expecting to hear your voice in this moment. Open my heart and my mind to experience and hear your truth in a new way. I lay my wounds and brokenness before you, in hope and anticipation that you will heal it all. May I hear new revelation this week! May I see you and your truth in a new light! Wrap your grace around me and speak softly to your daughter. I am here to listen.

Amen.

Dear Jesus,

_____

_____

_____

_____

_____

_____

_____

Immanuel

"Therefore the Lord himself will give you a sign: The virgin will conceive and give birth to a son, and will call him Immanuel."

Isaiah 7:14

We have learned that the Old Testament functioned out of a law based system of interaction with God. Obedience to the law meant that God was with you. And when He was with you, you knew that you would have victory. You knew that nothing, absolutely no king, no army, no force could win against you. Every battle fought, every famine experienced, every enemy that came against you, could be overturned by the gloriously divine advantage. When God was with you; you knew you could face anything.

This passage of Isaiah prophesied to Jesus' coming. What is interesting is the name Jesus' is called: Immanuel. Immanuel literally means "God with us." Jesus was fully human but He was also fully God. When Jesus came to earth, He was bringing the very presence of God with Him. God walked in and among humanity; He was with us! When Jesus died to cancel our sin debt, He pushed the gates wide open, allowing the Holy Spirit to enter our lives; so that we can live in the presence of "God with us" at all times!

We have the gloriously divine advantage with us everywhere we go at every moment of the day. And just like the Israelites could face every battle, every famine, every hardship with certainty that God would give them victory, we too can face every point of opposition with that same boldness. This concept is so difficult for us to grasp. Surrounded by constant failure and oppression, our eyes are blinded to the world of triumph that God intends for His people. This truth will change your life if you let it; if you allow God's all-powerful, all-consuming, ever-conquering Spirit flow over your heart and mind.

Let the assurance of God's victory in every area of your life overwhelm you. Let Jesus speak into those battles with His vanquishing Spirit. What specific battles have you been trying to face on your own and what is Jesus speaking to you about them?

The Holy Collision

"In the beginning was the Word, and the Word was with God, and the Word was God..." "The Word became flesh and made his dwelling among us. We have seen his glory, the glory of the one and only Son, who came from the Father, full of grace and truth."

John 1:1 & 14

Logos. A Greek word that not many Christians talk about. But it holds extreme significance. It literally means the "word." Jesus was the divine "logos;" the living, breathing, human form of the word of God. Can you literally imagine that? Jesus fulfilled all laws, lived up to every command and could not sin because He was the living law! He was the prime example of the law lived out in perfection through human hands.

John describes in his gospel the collision of a holy God and an unholy people. But the absolute majesty of God is that He did it in one person. Jesus was fully human; He could feel and experience everything we do. But He was also fully God, therefore acting and reacting in complete holiness. Through Jesus, the perfect limitless God was brought into a stained and tainted humanity.

As we learned last week, the divide between fallen humanity and a perfect God is incomprehensible. And yet God bridged this colossal gap in one person! Not with you, not with me, but with Jesus. Jesus joined the holy and the human together again. He reunited creator and creation. He married God and His people once again, for all eternity. As Ephesians 1 says, Jesus came "to bring unity to all things in heaven and on earth under Christ." Jesus is our unifier and umbrella. He brings us into the presence of God and through His covering we are made blameless.

Imagine the life of Jesus; being the living "Logos." How would you respond if you could interact with the living word of God?

_____

_____

_____

_____

_____

_____

_____

_____

_____

_____

_____

_____

_____

_____

_____

_____

_____

_____

_____

_____

Fullness of Holiness

> "And the child grew and became strong; he was filled with wisdom, and the grace of God was on him."
>
> **Luke 2:40**
>
> "We have seen his glory, the glory of the one and only Son who came from the Father, full of grace and truth." "Out of his fullness we have all received grace in place of grace already given."
>
> **John 1:14b, 16**

Jesus was the fullness of the law. But He was even more than just the divine "logos"- He was completely saturated in grace and truth. But what does that even mean? We throw around those words, "grace and truth," as if we know what they mean, but what weight do they truly hold?

Grace is a word that carries a profound depth of meaning; it means loving kindness, favor, joy, delight, loveliness, knowledge and affection. It is a force that strengthens faith and supernaturally gives people the desire to live out God's law. *Truth* is the freedom from falsehood and deceit. It is reality; infallible and verifiable nature. So all of that is in the one person of Jesus. In Him there is no falsehood or deceit, only justice, loving-kindness, good desires, faith and blessing.

Jesus was the perfect picture of true love and grace. When John wrote about "grace upon grace" or "grace in place of grace," we can also say that as "love in place of love." God loved His people unconditionally, but that love was made complete, made whole and displayed most fully in the person of Jesus Christ. He replaced the old system of conditional favor with a relationship of unconditional love.

When Jesus died on the cross, He was ultimately giving us the opportunity to have the fullness of grace and truth as well. Through His sacrifice he was able to open the flood gates for us to experience pure love, delight, joy, knowledge and favor. On top of that, He is able to grant us supernatural faith and the desire to obey God's will. Greater yet, His blood gives us access to His truth; the truth that exposes our wounds and sin so that He can then change, mold and heal us. In His holy truth we can combat every lie that Satan feeds us and every sin that has held us down. That is the power and fullness of grace and truth.

Meditate on the words "grace and truth." Knowing the power that those words have and how they are placed within you, how does that change how you view your identity in Jesus?

_____

_____

_____

_____

_____

_____

_____

_____

_____

_____

_____

_____

_____

_____

_____

_____

_____

_____

Every Single One

> "The law of Moses was unable to save us because of the weakness of our sinful nature. So God did what the law could not do. He sent his own Son in a body like the bodies we sinners have. And in that body God declared an end to sin's control over us by giving his Son as a sacrifice for our sins. He did this so that the just requirement of the law would be fully satisfied for us, who no longer follow our sinful nature but instead follow the Spirit."
>
> **Romans 8:3-4**
> *(New Living Translation)*

There is so much truth packed into these two verses; but focus in on the last line- "he did this so that the just requirement of the law would be fully satisfied for us." Remember, Jesus was the fulfillment of God's law. He was the perfect example of grace and truth in human form. And because Jesus was the bridge between us and God, His death held profound meaning!

When we go back to Old Testament scripture, we see that in order for sin to be forgiven the blood of an innocent animal had to be spilt. But those animals were just the temporary covering for humanity's sin. Jesus was the perfect sacrifice. His innocent blood covers our sin completely and permanently.

Upon the cross Jesus satisfied the whole law. He took upon Himself all of our sin while we did not even have the strength to lay our sin before Him. Jesus fulfilled each and every commandment and wiped away each and every single sin (past, present and future), paying the price to clear our sin debt.

I have caught myself from time to time hoarding my own sin. I think that "this part of my past" or "this habit" or even "this mistake" is too dirty for God. I hoard my mess, and therefore I heap up guilt and shame which consume my mind, all centered around these sins that are simply "too filthy" for Jesus to forgive. But the truth of the gospel- the profound reality of Jesus- is that nothing we have done is too far gone for Him to pardon. The gravity of that principle is impossible for most of us to comprehend. We feel as though we have to feel some shame, or that we should rub our own noses in our mess. But God says, "Let me free you from all this; let me make you free indeed." Jesus paid our ransom, so He could unlock every shackle that holds us down. Every single one.

What are the sins in your life that you see as "too dirty" for God? What shackles are still holding you down from true freedom in Jesus?

_____

_____

_____

_____

_____

_____

_____

_____

_____

_____

_____

_____

_____

_____

_____

_____

_____

_____

_____

_____

_____

Better

> "The former regulation is set aside because it was weak and useless (for the law made nothing perfect), and a better hope is introduced, by which we draw near to God." "...Jesus has become the guarantor of a better covenant," "But because Jesus lives forever, he has a permanent priesthood. Therefore he is able to save completely those who come to God through him, because he always lives to intercede for them."
>
> **Hebrews 7:18-19 & 22 & 24-25**

The Israelites and God worked together through a series of covenants. This legal binding agreement made sure that both parties fulfilled their end of the deal. When we discuss covenantal language, we aren't talking like a pinky promise between elementary schoolmates. We are talking serious business. God is true to His word- He is always faithful, always true, and always upholds His promises.

Up until this moment when Jesus entered the picture, the Israelites were expected to uphold a perfect life, and to keep their records completely clean. But here in Hebrews, a new agreement is set up and its terms are simple: Jesus. That's it. Jesus is the new covenant. But He isn't just the new covenant; He is the better covenant. The word better in greek is "Kreitton." This literally means "more useful, more serviceable, more advantageous, more excellent".

The promise that Jesus' death and resurrection hold is far better than any covenant we ever had before. The law no longer holds any authority. Jesus has fulfilled those terms and has brought to us a better hope.

So what does that all mean to me? Covenant language is not relevant, right? Wrong. We need to accept that the old way of "religion" is no longer applicable to us. The "works" based religion, where "my good deeds" equals "right with God," is totally void. But some of us still operate out of that thinking. We need to wrap our minds around the fact that our faith is in Jesus and not our own works. He is the "more useful, more serviceable, more advantageous, more excellent" covenant. He is our hope, our promise for a better tomorrow, our covering that will forever pay our sin debt.

How do you find yourself operating out of the old covenant based on your good works? How does the promise of Jesus being the better covenant change your view of faith/ religion?

_____

_____

_____

_____

_____

_____

_____

_____

_____

_____

_____

_____

_____

_____

_____

_____

_____

_____

_____

Grace Stories

I grew up attending a Presbyterian Church and I continue to attend that same Presbyterian Church today. My twin sister, Jenni and I attended church services, Sunday school, and youth group. I knew of God but it wasn't until I was twelve in the summer of 1994 that I gave my life to Jesus and found my best friend. I remember sitting in the basement of our church on a table next to Jenni watching the rest of my youth group running around playing tag football. I remember thinking something isn't right and that something is missing. Now, I don't quite remember when I brought it up to my mom that I didn't feel I was getting what I should be out of the church youth group but I do remember our neighborhood friend Kim asked us to attend her church youth group to try it out. My mom was very supportive and was open to letting both Jenni and me try it. We went to Kim's church youth group and were then asked to attend their annual youth group lock in. At this lock in Bonnie, the youth group leader announced that she would award a bag of M&M's to whoever named three people we had just met that night. I really wanted those M&M's and was the first person up to Bonnie's office to claim my price. After all, everyone I met (aside from Jenni and Kim) were new people to me. Again, here is where God is clever and creative. I named two people and then I named myself! My explanation was that I felt like I was someone new and different. Right there in Bonnie's office with an older youth group member named Molly, I committed my life to God and started on a new journey. My parents were very supportive and understanding in letting my sister and me decide what youth group we wanted to continue to attend. We became a permanent part of that church youth group. In December of that same year we went as a youth group to a Christian convention where my sister gave her life to God and I attended my first altar call to again start my life and relationship with God. I am very blessed for that start of my walk with God and that foundation I have in Him.

Even though I would like to think my grace story started in 1994 it actually started before then because God is always and was always with me. It amazes me how creative God is and how blessed I really am. When my sister and I were born we were premature and weighed only two pounds. We were in the hospital, I believe, two months or so after we were born. Upon birth we were removed from the care of our birth parents and placed in the care of social services and needed to be placed in a foster home. How amazing our God is that the foster family we were eventually placed with had just decided to no longer take anymore foster children because it had gotten to be too much to handle emotionally. They decided to take Jenni and me as their last foster children. Jenni and I stayed with them until *they* adopted us at the age of four! How blessed that I stayed with the people we always knew as mom and dad and that Jenni and I stayed together through the whole process. I am very blessed for her and for the bond we have. I remember my mom telling me that when we were younger she was told by a psychologist that we would never graduate from High School. My mom never took that as a fact. And yes, there was and continues to be learning struggles, but that is part of who I am. We graduated from High School and I went on to graduate and receive a bachelor and master degree. I was bullied throughout my elementary, middle, and high school years. Those things have carried over into how I view myself today, so I can be my own worst enemy.

Throughout the years, especially middle and high school, I remember finding comfort in Him and knowing He loved me. What's funny is that I find I need to remember that truth more now than I did back then. It has not been easy but God knows what He is doing even if sometimes we cannot see it. He brings us those struggles and seasons for a reason to rely on Him and recognize those gifts and strengths He has placed within us. I don't know who I would be without my family, but I was never meant to. In this particular season I find strength in Him as I am trying to find out where He wants me to go. I struggle with my insecurities and those feelings of worthlessness and failure, but He loves ME, *He* accepts *me* and He does have a plan. I need to let go of the fear and lies that blind me and keep me stuck, to remember where it all started for me before I was even born, and allow His peace to settle in.

Julie

Weekly Reflection

Take a few moments to quiet yourself before the Lord. Find your comfy spot, or retreat to a place where you often meet with the Lord. In that place, allow your heart, mind and soul to rest into the presence of God. Turn off the distractions, put your to-do list away, and simply be in the present moment. This is your time to be transparent with the Lord, to lay before him your wounds, hurts and struggles, and lift up your requests and deepest desires. You may praise Him, sit in the stillness and listen, or cry to release pain or hurt. The only thing you need to be is real with your heavenly Papa. You may pray the prayer below, or dive into your own. May this time be a blessing to your heart; may the Lord speak to you in new ways; may you allow the comforting and healing hands of our Father reach out to you; and may you allow the peace and joy of the Holy Spirit to pour over you.

Lord Jesus,

I am expecting to hear your voice in this moment. Open my heart and my mind to experience and hear your truth in a new way. I lay my wounds and brokenness before you, in hope and anticipation that you will heal it all. May I hear new revelation this week! May I see you and your truth in a new light! Wrap your grace around me and speak softly to your daughter. I am here to listen.

Amen.

Dear Jesus,

Empty

> "For it is by grace you have been saved, through faith—and this is not from yourselves, it is the gift of God."
>
> ### Ephesians 2:8

At this point in the study, we have to consider where we fall into this picture of grace. We have learned about the fallen world, about Jesus' fullness and sacrifice, but where do we fit in that? Some people even get uncomfortable (probably the control freaks, like me) when we hear too much about grace and not enough about what we have to do in this whole deal. Well this is where you fit in.

Before you go on in this study you have to consider the fact that all of this-all of the scripture read, the teachings heard, and catchy churchy phrases-mean absolutely nothing if you don't believe any of it. No amount of Bible verses, sermons, worship songs, or wise counsel can change you unless you believe that it is all true. Every word written and spoken is absolutely void of any power until you place your faith in it.

It's exactly like an iPhone. It's great if you tell all your friends about your awesome phone, and you even say you believe that it works. You even take it out of the box for everyone to see, but then you never even turn it on to use it! You say you believe it works, but you don't actually attempt to use it.

If you only *say* you believe the scriptures, *tell* your friends about how awesome Jesus is, but then you never actually *place* your faith in Jesus and believe the truth that he is offering you, then all of these words are empty of all their potential power. I lived in this camp for a long time, saying that I believed in the power of the cross, that grace was in me, and that Jesus could heal, but when the rubber met the road, I never stepped out to trust that Jesus' promise was true. So before you go on, take some faith inventory. Where do you stand in all of this? Are all your words empty of power? Or are you stepping out to actually *use* the truth you've been given?

Have you found yourself saying you believe the Bible, but not yet actually not placed your faith in the truth? What is holding you back from believing the power of the Gospel?

_____

_____

_____

_____

_____

_____

_____

_____

_____

_____

_____

_____

_____

_____

_____

_____

_____

_____

More Faith

> "Therefore, since we have been justified through faith, we have peace
> with God through our Lord Jesus Christ, through whom we have
> gained access by faith into this grace in which we now stand.
> And we boast in the hope of the glory of God."
>
> **Romans 5:1-2**

One of my biggest struggles with faith is that I never know if I have "enough" of it. When I have gone through tough life situations in the past, sometimes people have told me to just "have more faith." But how do I even know when I've actually reached that level of "more faith?" What does one feel like when one has enough faith?

The trouble is that faith isn't a tangible or physically measurable part of our life. We can't step on a scale and have it tell us if we have enough faith that day. There isn't any thermometer that can tell us if we have "healthy" faith temperature. But what if faith wasn't as complicated as we have made it out to be?

Hebrews 1:1 defines faith as "being sure of what we hope for and certain of what we do not see." Faith has nothing to do with our feelings. It is not wavering or unstable. Faith is assurance, steadfastness and confidence, a solid rock as a foundation. Faith is simply about surrender. It's about realizing that you can't earn grace by what you do and you can't lose grace because of what you do. Faith has nothing to do with you and everything to do with the certainty and solid cornerstone of Jesus Christ.

When we accept the gift of God; when we believe in the sacrifice of Jesus Christ, it comes down to a single question- do you have faith *or not?* You either have faith that Jesus is who He says he is and will do everything He says He will do, or you don't. You either surrender your life to Him or you don't. It's just that simple. You can't have "more faith" or "less faith." If you place your trust in Jesus Christ, He is your rock and your foundation. If you place your faith in Jesus, let Him be God in your life, let Him be the rock upon which you stand. He will never demand any more faith from you, but rather hope that you surrender everything to Him.

What does your struggle look like to just "have more Faith"? Have you surrendered everything to Jesus? Have you placed your faith, completely and truly, in Him?

One Groom

"But now, by dying to what once bound us, we have been released
from the law so that we serve in the new way of the spirit,
and not in the old way of the written code."

Romans 7:6

R ead Romans 7:1-6. It's a lot of imagery. But let's break it down to its bare bones. We read about the image of marriage. We learn that we can only be married to one groom- either the law or grace. We can't serve both Christ, who gives us grace, and also try to merit grace through our works. We have either died to the law through Christ or follow the law completely.

I think a lot of times in the church community we live out this example of having two grooms. We place a yoke over people, expecting them to live up to this standard of holiness and Godliness. And in the same breath we hear about God's grace and how he covers all sins. I don't know about you, but that double message confuses the living daylights out of me! Am I under grace or am I under a law? Am I supposed to live up to a Christian standard, or am I free under Christ's sacrifice?

I'm not sure about you, but once I'm under that law, it only makes me want to rebel. If you tell me I can't swear, you can only guess what I'm gonna do! But the beauty of living under grace is that we are free to love Jesus completely and wholly. Remember last week when we learned that grace places the desire to obey God's command within your heart! So, no longer are you under the obligation to live this way or act that way; the holiness of God and imitation of Jesus Christ flows through your life because you are passionately in love with Jesus and you are fully accepted under the freedom of grace.

Maybe at this point you need to choose your groom. Are you married to the law? Or to grace? When you are married to grace, the law is not only dead, but you are free to be in love with Jesus and let His love transform your life.

Have you found yourself married to two grooms? Does the love of Jesus seem too good to be true? Write down your love letter to Jesus. What is on your heart about His love for you?

By Works

> "And if by grace, then it cannot be based on works; if it were, grace
> would no longer be grace."
>
> **Romans 11:6**

There is no middle road with faith versus works- we have firmly established that truth this week. But I think we have to keep hammering it home because it is such a deeply rooted lie in so many of us. Our natural tendency is to want to bring something to the table for our relationships. Take me, for example. Through my own broken past of crazy terrible relationships, I have been trained to give everything and expect nothing in return. It has been nearly impossible for me to accept love and service from other people, and yet at the end of the day I feel as though I have to give everything I have to keep that person around. I have learned this terrible habit of "love scales," meaning if you do something nice for me then I have to do something nice for you. If you buy me a gift, then I have to up the ante and buy you a more expensive gift. Anyone feel me on this?

We often see Jesus through the vision of these "love scales." He died for us, therefore there has to be something that we can do for Him. In fact, when we grasp the fact that He died for us, the greatest gift ever, we feel this pressure to up the ante and do something for Him that is better than that gift!

Rest today knowing that Jesus doesn't expect a greater gift from you. He isn't impatiently waiting for you to return the favor or do something out of this world to show that you love Him. His joy comes from the fact that you can't do anything to make Him love you more or less. His love is pure without any corrupt motives. He is simply waiting for you to accept that there is nothing you can do to change that fact. Grace is grace; He gives it freely and expects absolutely nothing in return.

Are you stuck in the battle between accepting Jesus' love and yet wanting to pay Him back for what He has done? Or do you feel as if you have to live up to a standard to keep that love? What is Jesus speaking to you about that battle?

_____

_____

_____

_____

_____

_____

_____

_____

_____

_____

_____

_____

_____

_____

_____

_____

_____

_____

Walk it Out

"'Lord, if it's you,' Peter replied, 'tell me to come to you on the water.'
'Come,' he said. Then Peter got down out of the boat, walked on the
water and came toward Jesus. But when he saw the wind, he was afraid
and, beginning to sink, cried out, 'Lord, save me!'"
Matthew 14:28-30

Find a quiet place to be alone before the Lord. I want you to imagine yourself in this story of Peter and Jesus, truly imagine yourself in the perspective of one of the characters. Now read the whole story in Matthew 14:22-33.

This passage is the perfect picture of faith and trust. When Peter stepped out of the boat onto the water, he could not have just a little faith. He had to believe completely, he either trusted or didn't trust, he either walked or sank. There was no middle ground.

This same imagery applies to our own walk with Jesus. When we step out of the boat, that is a step of faith. But from there we choose if we trust God with each step, if we have faith in His promises and believe that He is who He says He is and will do everything He promised He would do. But we can also choose to focus on the storms around us. We can choose to set our sights on our brokenness, our persecution, our bad habits, our situations, our one sin that we can't seem to shake. In that moment when we choose to take our eyes off of Jesus that we will begin sinking in our muck.

The beautiful part about this picture is that as fast as Peter doubted Jesus' power, Jesus was there to help him back up. Jesus wasn't waiting for Peter to fall and He wasn't waiting to condemn him for doubting. But rather, He was patiently waiting to help Peter back up.

Now read the passage again. This time, imagine the steadfast and loving gaze of Jesus as you walk toward Him. Don't take your eyes off of Him. That is the picture of us walking toward a healed and restored life in Jesus.

Write about what you saw in this exercise. What was Jesus saying to you about having faith and keeping your gaze fixed on Him?

_____

_____

_____

_____

_____

_____

_____

_____

_____

_____

_____

_____

_____

_____

_____

_____

_____

_____

Grace Stories

My husband and I have been married for 5 years now and have seen first-hand God's Grace for us individually and as a couple. Just the day-to-day blessings He has placed upon our marriage and lives are proof that His Grace is sufficient. After about 2 years of marriage we began the journey to start a family. This has been one of the hardest most frustrating things I have ever experienced. It is difficult to put into the words how one feels when you long for something so badly and not have it happen.

After about 1-2 years of trying is when the bitterness and frustration really started to affect me. I found myself getting angry and sad when others would announce a pregnancy or birth. I thought to myself, "How awful am I to be upset with one of the most amazing miracles and blessings a couple could have?" It. Is. Hard. I have had a difficult time with the generic empty responses from friends when all you really want to hear is, "I can't imagine what you're going though. You're right, this sucks!"

You are probably expecting a big dramatic ending to my story including an announcement that we are pregnant, but I'm sorry to disappoint. My story isn't finished. And that is ok. The man after God's own heart, David, expresses this more than once in the Psalms. I don't know what the future holds, but God knows the desires of my heart and I have learned to not only lean on His understanding but to also look back and see His faithfulness and grace throughout my life. I find comfort in His unchanging Word. The Apostle Paul in Ephesians 3:14-21 writes, "Now to him, who is able to do far more abundantly than all that we ask or think according to the power at work in us..." And in Philippians 4:7 he writes, "...and the Peace of God, which surpasses all understanding, will guard your hearts and your minds in Christ Jesus." That last verse is the only way I can explain how I have not succumbed to a deep depression through this season. He has literally placed a peace of understanding on my heart and mind even though I have nothing tangible to show for it. God indeed has and will continue to be my rock, my refuge and very strong fortress!

Elizabeth

Weekly Reflection

Take a few moments to quiet yourself before the Lord. Find your comfy spot, or retreat to a place where you often meet with the Lord. In that place, allow your heart, mind and soul to rest into the presence of God. Turn off the distractions, put your to-do list away, and simply be in the present moment. This is your time to be transparent with the Lord, to lay before him your wounds, hurts and struggles, and lift up your requests and deepest desires. You may praise Him, sit in the stillness and listen, or cry to release pain or hurt. The only thing you need to be is real with your heavenly Papa. You may pray the prayer below, or dive into your own. May this time be a blessing to your heart; may the Lord speak to you in new ways; may you allow the comforting and healing hands of our Father reach out to you; and may you allow the peace and joy of the Holy Spirit to pour over you.

Lord Jesus,

I am expecting to hear your voice in this moment. Open my heart and my mind to experience and hear your truth in a new way. I lay my wounds and brokenness before you, in hope and anticipation that you will heal it all. May I hear new revelation this week! May I see you and your truth in a new light! Wrap your grace around me and speak softly to your daughter. I am here to listen.

Amen.

Dear Jesus,

_____

_____

_____

_____

_____

_____

_____

Became to Become

> "God made him who knew no sin to be sin for us, so that in him we might become the righteousness of God."
>
> **2 Corinthians 5:21**

This verse literally sums up the entire gospel for us. But what I love about these words is that it focuses on a completely different side of the gospel. For so many of us we read the "first half" of the gospel's message; that we are forgiven from sin. And then we stop there. We read "God made him who knew no sin to be sin for us" and we stop dead in our tracks. We then mediate on all of our sin that He had to bear for us.

We walk around then with this negative mentality, burying ourselves in the fact that we are sinners. We constantly throw around phrases like "I'm a sinner saved by grace" or "I'm just a forgiven sinner." But that mindset sends us into a tailspin and consistently reminds us of all the mistakes we've ever made or sins we've ever committed.

Jesus doesn't want us to walk around cemented in our sin. He doesn't want us water down the gospel to just simply being forgiven of sin. His death was more powerful than just wiping our slates clean.

Now for second part to the gospel message: Jesus became sin for us so that we could become the righteousness of God! We aren't just forgiven sinners or sinners saved by grace, we are the righteousness of God! That changes everything in our lives. Righteousness changes who we are, what we stand for and how we stand with God. It holds the ability to change everything in your life. In Christ you are not just forgiven, but you are righteously redeemed.

When we accept this truth, we can walk around focusing not on the mess of our life, but on the blessing of being redeemed in Christ. Now *that* is a change in perspective!

Do you see yourself as simply a forgiven sinner or righteously redeemed? How have you viewed yourself in the past, and what is Jesus telling you about your identity through His grace?

_____

_____

_____

_____

_____

_____

_____

_____

_____

_____

_____

_____

_____

_____

_____

_____

_____

Face to Face

"Therefore, since we have been justified through faith, we have peace
with God through our Lord Jesus Christ, through whom we have
gained access by faith into this grace in which we now stand.
And we boast in the hope of the glory of God."

Romans 5:1-2

Yesterday we talked about righteousness. That is a very heavy theological word, one that most people don't understand in the least. So many times growing up, I heard that I was righteous, and had no clue what that meant for my own life.

When we look at this verse in Romans we read the phrase "we have peace with God." The word "with" in that phrase is the Greek word "pros" which literally means "face to face 'with'."

All throughout the Old Testament, the Israelites were not able to even look upon the face of God. After they were cast out of the garden they no longer had the open relationship with God to be in His midst, let alone see His face! If any person even set foot into the holy of holies where the presence of God dwelled with a single blemish or uncleanliness on them, they would literally be killed on the spot! The Israelites would even have to tie a rope to individuals walking into that room to make sure they could bring them back out in case they died!

But Jesus undoes all of that. Through His sacrifice He literally gives us the ability to see God face to face again. That is something that only Jesus can do; only He could put us back together with our creator to be in a face to face relationship again.

That is the picture of righteousness. Because of sin we were unworthy to even be in the presence of God, and now through Jesus' blood, we are able to step confidently into the holy of holies to look upon the face of our God and King.

How does this picture of righteousness affect you? How does this perspective of righteousness change your view of grace and the power of Jesus' death?

_____

_____

_____

_____

_____

_____

_____

_____

_____

_____

_____

_____

_____

_____

_____

_____

_____

_____

_____

_____

_____

Right Standing

> "All this is from God, who reconciled us to himself through Christ and gave us the ministry of reconciliation: that God was reconciling the world to himself in Christ, not counting people's sins against them. And he has committed to us the message of reconciliation."
>
> **2 Corinthians 5:18-19**

Today we dive just a little deeper into the idea of righteousness. We read Paul's writing to the church in Corinth that we are reconciled, through Christ, to God. The word reconcile talks about the process of entities becoming compatible.

Before Jesus' death we were incompatible with God. Humanity was tarnished by sin. God was all holy and perfectly pure. Those two bodies could not go together; it was like trying to mix oil and water.

But through Jesus we are made compatible with God. He reconciles, reunites and restores us back to right relationship with our Heavenly Father. When we take on the righteousness of God; when Jesus places the robe of righteousness over our shoulders, we can literally stand before God blameless and pure.

Therefore, the sin that made us unfit to be in the presence of God is thrown on the cross. Paul says it perfectly here that as God was reconciling the world to Himself, he was "not counting people's sins against them." That means that He literally casts those sins out of His own memory! The God who knows all things, the one who has seen everything you have ever done, and is the only one holy enough to judge you for your sin has literally thrown out all of the evidence! Each and every sin we commit is wiped with Jesus' blood and is erased before our God.

This idea completely rocked my world! To think that God chooses to forget my sin. I am placed in right standing before my God without any blemish or stain on me. But the funny thing was that while my God could forget my sin, I still let it linger in my mind. If the God of all the universe can chose to forget your sin, then you too must forget it. Don't let pardoned sin make you feel guilty when you have already been declared innocent.

What sins are you still holding onto and feeling guilty about? Is it difficult to accept that God chooses to remember your sins no more? Why?

_____

_____

_____

_____

_____

_____

_____

_____

_____

_____

_____

_____

_____

_____

_____

_____

_____

_____

_____

Heirs

> "To the one who is victorious, I will give the right to sit with me
> on my throne, just as I was victorious and sat down with
> my Father on his throne."
>
> **Revelation 3:21**

So far we have learned that we are made right with God through His only Son, Jesus. But we are not just reconciled to God to simply stand before Him. Ephesians 2:6 sums up our greater inheritance, "And God raised us up with Christ and seated us with Him in the heavenly realms in Christ Jesus, in order that in the coming ages he might show the incomparable riches of his grace, expressed in his kindness to us in Christ Jesus."

We are raised with Christ, and we are made blameless and holy; to rule and reign with Jesus! That is part of our monumental identity shift. Can you see why simply seeing ourselves as forgiven sinners falls incredibly short of what God intends for us? We are not saved to keep walking around in our ho-hum lives, with the stamp of sinner still on our foreheads. We have a new identity and a new place to sit- right next to Jesus! Our citizenship is no longer of this world. We no longer find our place in sin, guilt, shame, or condemnation. But now we can walk free from that frame of mind, and we can step into our new identity in Christ with all of the blessing and riches that He has designed to give us.

With the righteousness of God placed upon us we become heirs to His throne. We become sons and daughters of the mighty king. If you haven't already hashed your identity out with Christ, take time to do that now. Ask Jesus to tell you who you are in Him. Ask Him to show you where you truly belong, which is on the throne next to Him!

What is Jesus telling you about your identity in Him? Can you imagine yourself on the throne next to Jesus? How does that imagery change your view of yourself?

Voices

> "Now it is God who makes both us and you stand firm in Christ.
> He anointed us, set his seal of ownership on us; and put his Spirit in
> our hearts as a deposit, guaranteeing what is to come."
>
> **2 Corinthians 1:21-22**

When grace washes over us, it means we have a new Lord in our life. When we were dead in sin, we were ruled by our sinful flaws. We listened to our own hearts and did what we saw fit. Even more than that, we were ruled by things of this world, and that includes Satan. Before Jesus enters our life, we are still consumed by the debt of our sin. We still feel the weight of that payment holding us down from living a truly abundant life.

And then Jesus steps in and flips our whole world upside down. In that flip, we give the throne in our lives to Jesus, allowing Him to be king. And in that moment, Jesus does something glorious: He sets his seal of ownership on us. As a sign of that seal, He gives us the Holy Spirit, to work in us and guide us in allowing Jesus to be King in our life.

Even though we are consciously aware of the Spirit at work in us and therefore making us aware of who we belong to, we often forget that Jesus is on the throne. I am so guilty of this. Time and time again I listen to the voice of Satan, other people, and my own selfish nature. I allow them to feed me lies that go directly against my identity in Christ. I momentarily forget who is on the throne in my life and who I am in Jesus. I allow the things that once ruled my life to slowly creep back in. I listen to that lie that tells me I'm not worthy of being loved. I listen to my selfish nature that tells me that I should not forgive that person who hurt my feelings. And little by little I put to the back of my mind the anointing that is on me and the grace that empowers me.

Jesus clearly says who we are in this passage; we are anointed ones with the Spirit of God within us. We belong to the King of kings. Nothing else should take His place on the throne in our life.

What things have been creeping in to try to take Jesus' place on the throne in your life? What voices do you listen to other than the one of your Savior?

_____

_____

_____

_____

_____

_____

_____

_____

_____

_____

_____

_____

_____

_____

_____

_____

_____

_____

_____

_____

_____

So far, I think my story can best be summarized as a process of accepting and believing in God's love for me, and in turn, learning to embrace the person He's designed me to be. Throughout my childhood I struggled very much to find loyal friends. I would have a "best friend" for a few years, pour my heart into being a good friend to them, and then they would leave me – to chase after the "in-crowd," a boy, or to invest their hearts into 'worldly' things. This cycle has broken my heart up until our wedding day, when one of my last "best friends" ditched our wedding party last minute.

All the while, I struggled to accept my body as beautiful. I hated my freckles, my fair skin, dark hair, and my curves. I remember this one defining moment in fifth grade, when a group of boys had me stand up in the lunch room only to laugh at me and mock how I looked. I played it tough – but I was so broken inside after that for a very long time. As a result, the way I looked at myself was broken and ashamed.

In the midst of this cyclical rejection by people I loved and my dislike for my body, the Lord called me to follow Him in my sophomore year of high school. I grabbed hold of Him and tried to share the Gospel with everyone I knew. This, by no surprise, pushed more friends away, and boys wanted more than I would ever give them. I know it sounds dramatic but at the age of 17 I really believed I would be alone for the rest of my life – with a small voice in my mind saying; "you're unworthy of love."

God turned my world upside down just a few months later when I met Dan; my now husband of two years. He was everything my mom never pictured my husband to be; he didn't know Jesus, he smoked cigarettes & pot, and he wore the baggiest ripped-up jeans you've ever seen. The Lord spoke so clearly to me that this guy was really special. I shared the Gospel with him and over time Jesus transformed his life and my perspective on love.

With Dan supporting me and reminding me that I am beautiful, I've continued to face many struggles to find loyal friends who love Jesus. In February of 2012, the Lord spoke clearly to my family that we were to leave our church home of 20+ years to pursue a church that really embraced spreading the Gospel to people above all else. In the midst of this transition, all of my "church friends" of 10+ years rejected our decision to leave the church and pushed us out of their lives.

I feel like this moment is in many ways the culmination of God speaking to me and refining my heart, up until now. I was very sad and very broken. I kept hearing the Lord say, "You have all you need– Me. I will provide everything you need, even the love and acceptance that you need." The Lord pushed all of my hurts and pains of rejection in my life to the surface and slowly purged them from me. In many ways, I feel like I've been freed from the yoke of "a need for acceptance and love from others." The "need" for people to reciprocate love for me has, in a sense, enslaved my heart and kept it away from the redeeming love of Jesus. So in this climactic moment of rejection, the Lord broke my chains.

I need reminding everyday that the Lord is all that I need. That He provides the perfect love that I desire. My husband, my mother, my father, my sister, my brother and my friends can never provide this perfect love for me. I need to turn to Jesus, for His perfect love to wash over me, forgive me of my sins, heal my hurt and pain, and redeem my brokenness. Day by day, I hear Him more clearly and feel Him more closely – transforming my heart and my mind.

Since this time, the Lord has done great things! He has brought us to a new church home. We feel so fed, uplifted, and encouraged by the preaching and people we have met. The Lord has also led us to start a ministry with our web design business, to provide any Bible-believing church who requests help with a free church website. Day by day the Lord continues to teach me and my husband more about obedience and relying on Him for all of our needs; physical and emotional. The challenges can be stressful, but God's provision is exciting and strengthens our faith. Thank you Jesus for you intervention in my life, and walking beside me everyday – through thick and thin!

Jamie

Weekly Reflection

Take a few moments to quiet yourself before the Lord. Find your comfy spot, or retreat to a place where you often meet with the Lord. In that place, allow your heart, mind and soul to rest into the presence of God. Turn off the distractions, put your to-do list away, and simply be in the present moment. This is your time to be transparent with the Lord, to lay before him your wounds, hurts and struggles, and lift up your requests and deepest desires. You may praise Him, sit in the stillness and listen, or cry to release pain or hurt. The only thing you need to be is real with your heavenly Papa. You may pray the prayer below, or dive into your own. May this time be a blessing to your heart; may the Lord speak to you in new ways; may you allow the comforting and healing hands of our Father reach out to you; and may you allow the peace and joy of the Holy Spirit to pour over you.

Lord Jesus,

I am expecting to hear your voice in this moment. Open my heart and my mind to experience and hear your truth in a new way. I lay my wounds and brokenness before you, in hope and anticipation that you will heal it all. May I hear new revelation this week! May I see you and your truth in a new light! Wrap your grace around me and speak softly to your daughter. I am here to listen.

Amen.

Dear Jesus,

_____

_____

_____

_____

_____

_____

_____

The Silk Dress

"Therefore, if anyone is in Christ, the new creation has come:
The old has gone, and the new is here!"

2 Corinthians 5:17

God consistently touches upon this idea of becoming new in His word. All throughout scripture God talks about new songs to be sung. New covenants to be made. New mercies given each morning and new creations through His spirit. But why is it so important to become new? Why does God stress this idea of becoming new so often? Let's imagine for a second this scenario of becoming new to help us get a picture of what this looks like.

Imagine for a moment that it's Friday night. You have a hot date and you want to hit the gym before you get ready. You have an excellent work out (let's say a Zumba cardio session), and when you get home you are the definition of a hot mess. Your clothes are drenched in sweat, you are filthy, and you are just plain nasty smelling. Now at this moment it would never cross your mind to put on your gorgeous silk dress on top of all that nastiness. You of course are going to rip those clothes off, take a long hot shower, and get your mind and heart in date mode. At that point, when you are all clean, you can then put on your new dress that you just bought (on sale at your favorite store, of course)!

We see from this process that we can't put on new clothes until we take off the old. We never put on clean clothes without taking off the dirty ones first. This is the image of our new life in Christ. We cannot keep our old self and also take on a new self, it just doesn't work like that. When we receive Christ, by grace through faith, we are ripping off our old nature, and putting on the new nature of Christ. Even when we still feel like the old self, even when we feel like we are still the same old person, we have been made new. We have a new mind, a new spirit, a new nature and a new identity in Christ. We are now chosen, holy, saints of Jesus Christ.

How is your 'new nature' different from your 'old nature?'
Do you still feel like you are living from your old nature?
What part of your old nature do you feel like you just can't
shake?

_____

_____

_____

_____

_____

_____

_____

_____

_____

_____

_____

_____

_____

_____

_____

_____

_____

_____

The Hulk

"For you died, and your life is now hidden with Christ in God.
When Christ, who is your life, appears,
then you also will appear with him in glory."

Colossians 3:3-4

Have you seen the movie "The Hulk?" If you haven't, basically what happens is that the professor Dr. David Banner becomes contaminated with a chemical that changes his body chemistry and turns him into a giant angry indestructible monster. In the moments when he turns angry his body chemistry changes and he becomes utterly consumed by the green exterior of the Hulk and his mind is sent into "Hulk mode." But whether or not Dr. Banner was in "Hulk mode," the Hulk DNA was in him and it was now who he was.

Now scratch that and reverse it. Can you imagine yourself immersed in something so deeply that you no longer see yourself? Even more, others no longer see you but the thing you are immersed in. That is the image of becoming new in Christ.

When you accept grace by faith, your life becomes immersed in Christ. He is in you and around you, consuming and changing who you are to your very core. But there are moments in our life when we don't feel as if we have changed at all. We see ourselves in the state of Dr. Banner, no hulk exterior, just plain old us.

But just like Dr. Banner still had the DNA of the hulk in him even in moments when he wasn't physically the hulk, we too still have the Spirit of Christ in us when we don't feel so Christ-like. Christ isn't just your Savior, your redeemer, a good man or one who gave His life for you, He is now your life. It is now Christ in you. It is now Christ enveloping you. You are surrounded and immersed in Jesus Christ. So now you operate out of Christ, because it is Him who is your substance and covering. Therefore you no longer walk out life, but Christ in you.

Imagine Christ in and around you. What feelings does this image trigger in you? Do you feel the spirit of confidence and security overwhelming you?

_____

_____

_____

_____

_____

_____

_____

_____

_____

_____

_____

_____

_____

_____

_____

_____

_____

_____

_____

Peanut M&Ms

"For the grace of God has appeared that offers salvation to all people. It teaches us to say "No" to unGodliness and worldly passions, and to live self-controlled, upright and Godly lives in this present age, while we wait for the blessed hope—the appearing of the glory of our great God and Savior, Jesus Christ, who gave himself for us to redeem us from all wickedness and to purify for himself a people that are his very own, eager to do what is good."

Titus 2:11-14

We can compare the fight between our old nature and new nature with an analogy that every woman has encountered: dieting. When we start a diet, we immediately think that we can't eat anything. Our minds go to the furthest extreme, "If I'm gonna lose this weight, I can't eat a single morsel!" And then your dear friend Jenny Sue so graciously brings a bag of M&Ms over to your house (and not just the regular M&Ms, but the peanut M&Ms!). Because you haven't eaten a single thing; your mouth immediately becomes a salivating vacuum and suddenly the bag is empty, and you have no idea what happened!

The reality of the situation is that you never should have starved yourself. Dieting isn't about starvation, but about changing the way you view food and making the right choices when you eat. The same goes for our Christian walk. Some people feel as though as soon as they become a Christian they have to become absolutely perfect. So they immediately cut out everything from their life and they no longer do anything! But then they see the giant bag of M&Ms and they lose all control.

The process of becoming more Christ-like isn't an instant change. Just like you won't lose ten pounds overnight from starving yourself, you can't change who you are and become magically perfect in one day. As the Spirit works to renew your mind, reshaping the way you think about life, you will learn to say no to certain habits and sins. God isn't one to point fingers and say, "Don't have any fun" or "Don't do anything." He is saying, "Let me slowly change and transform you into the beautiful image that I know you can be." Give yourself grace to enjoy the process of transformation. Our journey of faith is a day by day, moment by moment experience. Be steadfast each day in walking out your new nature, and rest in knowing that it is a process of becoming all that Christ desires for us to be.

With what situations or topics have you tried to become perfect overnight? What have been your "Peanut M&Ms?"

_____

_____

_____

_____

_____

_____

_____

_____

_____

_____

_____

_____

_____

_____

_____

_____

_____

_____

_____

_____

_____

Hampster Wheel

"For in Christ all the fullness of the Deity lives in bodily form,
and in Christ you have been brought to fullness.
He is the head over every power and authority."

Colossians 2:9-10

Have you ever felt the complete exhaustion from trying with all your might not to sin? You feel as though you are trying so hard, working painfully, tirelessly to be someone better and at the end of the day you made no progress.

Well, you're not moving forward because the mode of transportation you've chosen is a hamster wheel: you are going, going, going, running as fast as you can, but not getting anywhere. We try from our own strength, our own wisdom, our own will power to be the perfect Godly woman and then at the end of the day we are not only exhausted, but we're still stuck in the cage!

While it is impossible to be everything that God wants us to be by our own strength, there is hope! There is only one man who could completely live out the Christian life and that was Jesus Christ. We will never be able to fulfill every scripture and every command on our own. It is *impossible*. We are called to surrender everything. We are to let Him be Christ in and through us. Christ is the fullness of grace and truth; and all of that is now in you!

Colossians 1:27 sums it up perfectly, "To them God has chosen to make known among the Gentiles the glorious riches of this mystery, which is Christ in you, the hope of glory." Therefore now when we live, it is Christ in us, the hope of glory. We no longer have to depend on our own strength, will power or wisdom.

Jesus lives inside of you. It is Him that does all of the work in you to make us all that He wants you to be. You can't do anything by your own strength to "be better." It is all Him! And that is a glorious weight off your shoulders.

What does it look like to you to have Jesus Christ, the hope of glory, working within and through you? How does it affect your heart to know that it is Christ who is transforming you?

_____

_____

_____

_____

_____

_____

_____

_____

_____

_____

_____

_____

_____

_____

_____

_____

_____

_____

Never Never

> "Let your character or moral disposition be free from love of money [including greed, avarice, lust, and craving for earthly possessions] and be satisfied with your present [circumstances and with what you have]; for He [God] Himself has said, I will not in any way fail you nor give you up nor leave you without support. [I will] not,[I will] not, [I will] not in any degree leave you helpless nor forsake nor let [you] down (relax My hold on you)! [Assuredly not!]."
>
> **Hebrews 13:5** *(Amplified Version-Classic Edition)*

You did that *one thing* you promised God before that if He got you out of it, you would never do again. But once more you find yourself on your knees wondering how in the world you got here. You then follow the natural progression of youth camp and church: you rededicate your life, once again promising that you will never do this one thing again.

In those moments when you feel like garbage, absolutely distraught because you just can't get it together, you are only seeing yourself through the lens of your sin. You see the terrible mess you've made. You see the cloud of sin looming all around you, and it becomes all you can see.

But God sees through that cloud. In fact, when He looks at you, His daughter, all He sees is His Son. He doesn't even see the mess you've made; His loving gaze sees you seeing the majesty and beauty of His forgiven and righteous daughter. God isn't up in heaven keeping a tally of how many sins you've committed or how many times you've failed. God isn't waiting for you to rededicate your life again; to finally get things right. He is waiting for that moment that you simply hand every struggle, every temptation over to Him. And in those moments when you feel like an utter failure, just sitting in the mess you've made, Jesus is ready to dust you off and help you stand back up. Will you let Him?

Does this amplified version of scripture hit you right in the heart? God will never leave you or abandon you. He will not! He is not waiting for strike three to call you out. He is always waiting with open arms ready to embrace his beautiful and holy daughter.

Do you believe that God will truly never leave you, or have past experiences led you to believe otherwise? Write out your heart to God about His faithful nature.

_____

_____

_____

_____

_____

_____

_____

_____

_____

_____

_____

_____

_____

_____

_____

_____

_____

_____

Being raised in a Christian family, the name of Jesus was not foreign to me. I knew that Jesus was God's son. I knew that He died for my sins. I knew we were to love Jesus and I said that I loved Him. However, when you're a child, your faith doesn't seem to be challenged too much until something big happens in your life. That is where my grace story begins. When I was nearly two years old, my mom passed away from a brain tumor. I didn't get much of a chance to know who she was, and as a result, my dad became everything to me. He was my provider. My dad became both a mother and a father, and for all essential purposes, he was my God. He was my world. I didn't realize as an adolescent that God was just waiting for me on the sideline. God was not number one in my heart. My dad had filled that spot, or so I thought. When I turned 12 years old, my dad remarried. I didn't realize how terrible I was at sharing his attention and love. Let's just say I didn't make life easy for my new stepmom. We didn't always see eye to eye and it often caused friction in our family. Through some very turbulent times, I felt like my dad had let me down, abandoned me and couldn't stand up for me the way I "thought" he should. In my finite perspective, I felt like I had lost the person closest to me. After many years of tears and inner frustrations, God made it very clear that I needed to reach out to him. God brought me to a place where I thought I just couldn't go on. Little did I know that He was calling me to rely solely on Him. So I finally did.

In doing so, I realized that every human is imperfect. I was imperfect; my step-mom was imperfect; and even my dad was indeed imperfect. He couldn't be everything for me, nor should he. No matter how many ways we desperately try to fill our hearts with human love or possessions, we will never feel completely fulfilled. There will always be a hole in our hearts. That hole is only filled by Jesus. One night in my freshman year of college, I knelt before my bed. Feeling completely desperate, I asked God to be MY EVERYTHING. I knew I had found the person I could be fully reliant on: Jesus. I asked God to forgive me and to let Christ come in to my heart. Christ has forever changed me. My relationship with my stepmom has improved a lot. My dad is not my everything but he is still very special to me. My confidence in the Lord has only grown and grown. I have truly learned what it means to let your satisfaction come from God and God alone. He is my source of joy, security and peace. God's love is unfailing, unconditional and eternal. He positioned me in a spot where I could see Him move in my life. I am forever thankful.

Amy

Weekly Reflection

Take a few moments to quiet yourself before the Lord. Find your comfy spot, or retreat to a place where you often meet with the Lord. In that place, allow your heart, mind and soul to rest into the presence of God. Turn off the distractions, put your to-do list away, and simply be in the present moment. This is your time to be transparent with the Lord, to lay before him your wounds, hurts and struggles, and lift up your requests and deepest desires. You may praise Him, sit in the stillness and listen, or cry to release pain or hurt. The only thing you need to be is real with your heavenly Papa. You may pray the prayer below, or dive into your own. May this time be a blessing to your heart; may the Lord speak to you in new ways; may you allow the comforting and healing hands of our Father reach out to you; and may you allow the peace and joy of the Holy Spirit to pour over you.

Lord Jesus,

I am expecting to hear your voice in this moment. Open my heart and my mind to experience and hear your truth in a new way. I lay my wounds and brokenness before you, in hope and anticipation that you will heal it all. May I hear new revelation this week! May I see you and your truth in a new light! Wrap your grace around me and speak softly to your daughter. I am here to listen.

Amen.

Dear Jesus,

_____

_____

_____

_____

_____

_____

_____

Dirty Laundry

"You were taught, with regard to you former way of life, to put off your old self, which is being corrupted by its deceitful desires; to be made new in the attitude of your minds; and to put on the new self, created to be like God in true righteousness and holiness."

Ephesians 4:22-24

We are going back to date night one more time. We imagined the metaphor of taking off our dirty, nasty, sweaty clothes and putting on a beautiful silk dress, being like changing our old nature into a new nature. But today we are getting specific. We need to zero in on that metaphor because I don't think that many of us actually ever "put to death" our old self. Or rather, many of us still operate out of our old mindset even though we are made new! We use generalities so much in our faith; we say that we are made new, with new desires, new passion and new life. But we often don't get specific enough to actually call out what we are laying before Jesus. As we work through our wounds and our brokenness, we have to pinpoint the places where we are tainted. We have to hone in on the sins that we carry shame for. We have to call out the lies that Satan is still feeding us about ourselves. We must lay bare our wounds for Jesus to see.

It is in that moment when we call Satan out, or explain out loud the moment when we were inflicted with our deepest wound, or finally let out our greatest fears and doubts, that we disarm Satan's attempts to keep us in our mess. We call it for what it is: Satan no longer has authority over us. Therefore our sins, our old self, our brokenness and wounds are all under the loving grace and power of Jesus Christ.

So today call out what you are working through. What burdens are you carrying from your old self? What sins do you still feel guilt and shame for? What wounds are still open in you that need Jesus' touch? If you can, go back to the very moments when you gained these battle wounds. Lay it all out, take it off your shoulders and place it before the cross.

List here the wounds, sins, and moments that still linger in your heart and mind. Ask Jesus to heal these wounds.

_____

_____

_____

_____

_____

_____

_____

_____

_____

_____

_____

_____

_____

_____

_____

_____

_____

_____

_____

Bear Hugs

"But while he was still a long way off, his father saw him and was filled with compassion for him; he ran to his son, threw his arms around him and kissed him. "The son said to him, 'Father, I have sinned against heaven and against you. I am no longer worthy to be called your son.' "But the father said to his servants, 'Quick! Bring the best robe and put it on him. Put a ring on his finger and sandals on his feet. Bring the fattened calf and kill it. Let's have a feast and celebrate. For this son of mine was dead and is alive again; he was lost and is found.' So they began to celebrate."

Luke 15:20-24

Read the whole story of the prodigal son; Luke 15:11-31. It's a beautiful picture isn't it? We read that the son, after turning his back against his father, chose to take his inheritance and run, he ended up in such a desperate situation that while he was hired to feed pigs he longed to eat their food! The son, with his shoulders slumped, headed home, just hoping for a chance to be one of his father's servants.

And then we see the return of the son. This picture of the father's reaction is absolutely breathtaking. Imagine the father's face seeing his son come home. I can picture him jumping up and down, running to his son that he hasn't seen in what probably seemed like forever. He scoops him up with a gigantic bear hug and screams with joy at the top of his lungs that his son that was once lost is finally home! What a magnificent scene!

That's the image of grace for us. We often feel like this son when we sin: ashamed, far from God and defeated. It's those negative emotions that keep us separated from God for days, weeks, months or possibly even years! We feel as if we have sinned so terribly that He would never want to see our face again. After pouring out the sins that our heart still holds on to yesterday, it is so easy for Satan to now use that list against us. It would be easy for Him to now tell us that our list is too long, too bad and too dirty to forgive, but God is waiting for our return just like this father. He wants to scoop us up, clean us off and place a gorgeous robe around us. He isn't waiting to read off our sins or punish us for our rebellion. He only desperately longs to have us back in His arms again.

Can you imagine yourself in this scene? Can you imagine Jesus longing to embrace you after you have sinned, ready to scoop you up, and spend time with His beloved daughter? When He scoops you up, what is He whispering in your ear?

_____

_____

_____

_____

_____

_____

_____

_____

_____

_____

_____

_____

_____

_____

_____

_____

_____

Preach It

> "For he chose us in him before the creation of the world to be holy
> and blameless in his sight. In love he predestined us for adoption to
> sonship through Jesus Christ, in accordance with his pleasure and
> will–to the praise of his glorious grace; which he has freely given us
> in the One he loves."
>
> **Ephesians 1:4-6**

I have been a Christian for as long as I can remember; and yet there are still moments when I just don't feel as though I am God's daughter. There are moments when I feel just "blah" and like the weight of everything that I am (or everything I'm not!) is resting on my shoulders. Have you ever had those moments?

A technique I have learned when I'm in those "blah" moments is to preach to myself. Yes, I literally preach to myself. I have found that the moment I speak out loud God's word, the moment I declare the truth in the sound waves I begin to feel energized. My attitude and mood start to change, and often I end up so pumped up, excited and so invigorated with truth that I am literally shouting and pounding on the wheel of my car (because usually my sermons take place while I'm driving). That dramatic shift in mood can only happen because of the immense power of God's living word!

So what message do you need to speak to yourself? That you are holy and blameless before God. You are a daughter of God! (Romans 8:15-17) You are God's righteousness, clothed in God's riches and mercy (2 Corinthians 5:21). You are God's chosen possession, made new in Christ to be a saint (1 Peter 2:9-10). Everything you have learned about grace is material for your message.

Now I know what you are thinking; "I'm not a preacher! I hate speaking in front of other people!" But I encourage you to try this just once; the next time you are in a "blah" moment, start preaching this message. Look up these scriptures and begin to claim these truths as your own! You will face times when Satan is on the attack; you will feel the pressure from Satan to think less of yourself and to fall back into who you once were. But in those moments, the best thing to do is to start declaring God's truth. It is His truth that disarms the weapons of Satan. It is His truth that stands forever, and it is His truth that gives you the courage, power and confidence to walk out in freedom.

Read the verses listed and write out what those promises mean to you. Think about the lies that Satan attacks you with. Now write out what your response of truth is and give yourself preaching material!

_____

_____

_____

_____

_____

_____

_____

_____

_____

_____

_____

_____

_____

_____

_____

_____

_____

_____

_____

_____

Sackcloth

"You turned my wailing into dancing; you removed my sackcloth and clothed me with joy, that my heart may sing your praises and not be silent. Lord my God, I will praise you forever."

Psalm 30:11-12

We all struggle with joy. We all experience those moments when life is simply unlovely. Oftentimes, we believe the lie that as soon as we become saved, life will feel like all butterflies and rainbows, and that no pain will happen and no suffering will come our way. But that just isn't the truth. In fact it's the furthest from the truth.

Scripture explains to us the circumstances in life: that it will include sorrow and trials. That we will endure hardship and suffering. But that isn't the end of the story. The image of grace isn't just about our identity and becoming right with God- it's a whole mind shift. We no longer have to stay in the gloom of despair; our life doesn't end at the trials. There is no longer a period at the end of death and depression. Now there is a pause and comma where we add the words, "but, Jesus..." There will be trials, *but Jesus* died and was resurrected and that resurrection is our greatest hope.

These verses from Psalm 30 give us the picture of life and trials. Sackcloth in the Old Testament was a sign of mourning. So when the Psalm says that God removed the sackcloth, it is saying that God replaced the spirit of despair with a spirit of joy. We can read this in light of Jesus; that through His death we have grace, we can now experience true joy and freedom because we are no longer bound to sin or brokenness.

Now, does this mean that life becomes easier? Nope. Does this mean that we won't have times when we feel miserable and depressed? No way. Does this mean that our battle against our broken nature won't be difficult or painful? I wish, but no. So what does this mean? It means that now there is hope! There is a solution! It means that we can see every situation, every emotion, every hardship, every moment of the painful process of healing through the lens of Jesus. It means that we cast every care upon the Lord, because He is faithful to us and grants us supernatural peace in the midst of stormy days.

In what areas/circumstances of your life do you need to remove the sackcloth of mourning to receive the joy of Jesus?

The Right Cement

> "And you also were included in Christ when you heard the message of truth, the gospel of your salvation. When you believed, you were marked in him with a seal, the promised Holy Spirit, who is a deposit guaranteeing our inheritance until the redemption of those who are God's possession–to the praise of his glory"
>
> **Ephesians 1:13-14**

Earlier in this study we discussed the question of how you saw yourself-Are you just a forgiven sinner or are you righteously redeemed? I want to revisit that idea after now being seven weeks into this study. Where are you at with that question? Is your heart grasping that you are much more than just a sinner saved by grace? Are you beginning to see a glimpse of what true grace is- the freedom and fulfillment of being in restored relationship with God?

We have to establish this foundation because in the coming weeks we will be exploring two things- the power of grace to heal and all the blessings that flow from grace. But we can't grasp the nature of those things until we are rooted and established in the pure, unconditional, passionate love that God has for us!

You, just as you are right now in this moment, with all your garbage and brokenness, are a miracle of God. You are not a nobody. God pointed you out, pursued you, and came after you so that He can do a miraculous work in you. You are the intricately crafted, finely woven, detailed work of God's hands.

Today, let that truth pour over your heart. Let that be the foundation that you are cemented in. Going forward into a redeemed life that Jesus has for us is difficult (wait, scratch that, impossible!) if we do not truly know and accept who we are in the eyes of God. Satan will use every weapon against you. He will bring out all forces to keep you in your cement. But if your cement is made up of the grace and truth of Jesus, then all Satan's punches below the belt are rendered useless.

Walk through psalm 139:13-18. Ask Jesus to let you see it with new eyes; to truly believe each word of that promise. Who are you in Christ? What type of cement are you stuck in?

_____

_____

_____

_____

_____

_____

_____

_____

_____

_____

_____

_____

_____

_____

_____

_____

_____

ere's just a piece of my story that has brought me to this point today! My life radically changed when I moved to Florida for what I thought was to teach kindergarten, but was really where I accepted Jesus Christ as my Lord and Savior. My intimate relationship with Jesus grew as I said yes to international missions. This summer I traveled to Rwanda and Uganda, Africa. One morning we were on a bus ride to a ministry site. On that bus I began to cry. I heard the Lord tell me to go home to NY to be closer to family. My response was to wipe my tears so no one would notice and I responded to the Lord by saying, "I am going home to visit in one week; if there is something else I am suppose to do you are going to have to make it very clear to me," because I really felt like I was doing the Lord's work in Florida.

Well a few hours later the Lord made clear what I needed to do. Our team had spent the morning ministering to 300 children at Return Ministry in Uganda. While we were there some of the team had the chance to carry water in large buckets from the local "stream" to the home where many of the village children would eat their only meal of the day. Although uphill, the walk from the stream to the home was short – between a quarter and a half a mile. If you call that short just for clean water! Something the older children, who told us they went for water around 10 times a day, were grateful for.

Later that day we were delivering 20 pound bags of dried beans and large bars of laundry soap we had purchased to families in the village. We navigated dirt paths and narrow plank bridges, skirted along side walls, and stepped carefully to avoid the mud puddles.

Then, the inevitable happened... It had to be me! I slipped and ended up calf deep in the mud. I looked at my friend, Sarah, for a minute, admittedly a bit unsure what to do. Here we were in the middle of the village with no real way to clean up. So, we started to move on. Suddenly one of the local women motioned us over. "No, momma, momma!" she cried and she grabbed her wash tub and a heavy jug of water that we now understood she had carried for more than a mile. Without a moment's hesitation, she filled the tub and motioned for me to come over to wash my feet. Once my feet were clean, the woman proceeded to dry my feet with her clean laundry and to wash my shoes. For those of us who live with clean water, we wouldn't have thought twice about turning on the faucet. But this woman selflessly gave all of the water she had to clean the feet of another. That afternoon we saw God as this woman gave all that she had to a stranger. I saw this selflessness over and over again in Africa. Where people had little, yet they joyfully gave all.

It was here that I realized I need to be less selfish. Although I felt I was doing the Lord's work in Florida I knew I needed to move back to New York to be closer to family. I knew I had to give up all that I had in order to have more of Jesus. Moving has been a huge adventure and I have been blessed by many friends and family in this transition. The Lord has truly been showering me with blessings as I continue to say yes to Him and walk by faith.

Jessica

Weekly Reflection

Take a few moments to quiet yourself before the Lord. Find your comfy spot, or retreat to a place where you often meet with the Lord. In that place, allow your heart, mind and soul to rest into the presence of God. Turn off the distractions, put your to-do list away, and simply be in the present moment. This is your time to be transparent with the Lord, to lay before him your wounds, hurts and struggles, and lift up your requests and deepest desires. You may praise Him, sit in the stillness and listen, or cry to release pain or hurt. The only thing you need to be is real with your heavenly Papa. You may pray the prayer below, or dive into your own. May this time be a blessing to your heart; may the Lord speak to you in new ways; may you allow the comforting and healing hands of our Father reach out to you; and may you allow the peace and joy of the Holy Spirit to pour over you.

Lord Jesus,

I am expecting to hear your voice in this moment. Open my heart and my mind to experience and hear your truth in a new way. I lay my wounds and brokenness before you, in hope and anticipation that you will heal it all. May I hear new revelation this week! May I see you and your truth in a new light! Wrap your grace around me and speak softly to your daughter. I am here to listen.

Amen.

Dear Jesus,

His Scars

> "They were startled and frightened, thinking they saw a ghost. He said
> to them, 'Why are you troubled, and why do doubts rise in your minds?
> Look at my hands and my feet. It is I myself! Touch me and
> see; a ghost does not have flesh and bones, as you see I have."
>
> **Luke 24:37-39**

Have you ever wondered why Jesus kept His scars after He resurrected from the dead? Has it ever crossed your mind why He would ever want to be reminded of that brutal day in His life? That day was filled with trauma, with massive amounts of betrayal, and unfathomable pain that was continuously inflicted upon His weak human body. Why would anyone want to remember such a day?

In this passage Jesus appears to the apostles after He is resurrected. Having never experienced a resurrection before, they are obviously a lil' freaked out! At first, they even thought it was a ghost in front of them, and they doubted that it is truly their friend Jesus. So Jesus, unshaken by their doubting hearts, stands in front of his closest friends, watches them tremble in fear, and He simply reaches out His wrists and invites them to feel the imprints of His scars. You see, Jesus' proof to the apostles that He was the same man who experienced that gruesome day, were His scars. Can you imagine that moment of gently feeling Jesus' scars? They are no longer tender to the touch, they no longer delicate points of pain, they no longer trigger the feelings of suffering or betrayal for Jesus. He eagerly holds out His wrists, with love and freedom in His eyes, wanting you to see and feel that His wounds are completely healed.

Jesus could have come back from the dead, in a resurrected body that was completely healed. If He could raise himself from the dead, you can bet He has the power to heal His own wounds. And yet, He chose to keep His scars. He did this because He wants to tell you the story of who He is. He wants to share the story of the pain He endured and the suffering He overcame. He wants to show you that He is now healed from it all. Jesus knows that scars were evidence of a healed wound. And He wants to show every person His scars that saved the world.

What would be your reaction to touching Jesus' scars on His wrists, feet and side? What feelings does that evoke in you?

The Hard Road

> "Three times I pleaded with the Lord to take it away from me.
> But he said to me, 'My grace is sufficient for you, for my power is made
> perfect in weakness. Therefore I will boast all the more gladly about my
> weaknesses, so that Christ's power may rest on me."
>
> **2 Corinthians 12:8-9**

L et's just throw it out there: I wish being a Christian was easy. Heck, sometimes I wish life was easy. But we all know that it isn't. It's hard to live in this world. It's even harder to be a Christian living in this world. On top of just living and surviving in this world, it's also hard knowing that Christ gives us the opportunity to be redeemed, restored, and to be whole. It's a long, exhausting road to become whole, and anyone who tells us otherwise is lying. It's beyond tough to relive hurtful moments. It's so difficult for us to simply push past our terrible habits. And it's near impossible to stand for what's right in a broken world with so many, many broken people. God is passionate about putting His children back together. About helping to heal each of His sons and daughters of his/her wounds and bound hearts, in order to bring out the shining, beautiful people that He knows they can be. But sometimes the road to get to that place of wholeness is excruciating.

When we think about the process of becoming whole, we first have to go back to the start of it all. To heal properly from our brokenness, and not just slap a bandage on a gushing gash, we have to go back to the root of all the pain, to the very moment when we were inflicted with that cut. It may sting like the dickens to reopen that wound- to go back and revisit all the emotions of that moment, but we have to know that the pain is worth the payoff. The momentary sting is worth the lasting healing.

Paul goes on to say, "For when I am weak, then I am strong." These moments of "weakness," the moments when we feel vulnerable, emotional and overwhelmed with pain, are the moments when God is working on us the most. It's like when we exercise- when we start to feel the burn of exhausted muscles, that is when our muscles are starting to change. It's uncomfortable, but necessary, or we remain the same out-of-shape people we were before. Be steadfast in the hard road of becoming whole, the reward is worth it!

Go back in your memory to the moments when you believe your wounds were inflicted. It may be a series of moments in your life that have accumulated to numerous tiny cuts, or it may be a single event causing a huge gash that has radically changed your life. Journal those moments and surrender them to Jesus.

_____

_____

_____

_____

_____

_____

_____

_____

_____

_____

_____

_____

_____

_____

_____

_____

Picture of Glory

"And God raised us up with Christ and seated us with him in
the heavenly realms in Christ Jesus, in order that in the coming ages
he might show the incomparable riches of his grace,
expressed in this kindness to us in Christ Jesus."

Ephesians 2:6-7

Jesus used His scars to tell the story of who He was. But He didn't use them to explain the agonizing day when He was mercilessly beaten and eventually killed. If this was the point of that story then Jesus would have kept his open wounds! The purpose of the scars were to tell about His glorious victory over death!

We all have wounds in our life. Some of us have gaping holes in our hearts from traumatic situations that we have lived through. Others have numerous tiny scratches from repeated instances of conflict. Some wounds have been open for years; others are more recently obtained. But no matter what the wounds look like- the shape, form, depth or age- we all still have them.

God's goal in our lives is to heal every single wound we have. Every. Single. One. He will bind our open gash with the strength of His spirit and will stitch our cuts with His grace. He wants to turn each and every wound of ours into an admirable and exquisite scar. Our God is a redeemer, He does not leave lost things lost or broken things broken. He brings it all back to perfection.

As God heals you, and as you are gracefully freed from bondage and lies, you will gain a battle scar. But it will no longer be tender to the touch, or bring pain to your heart. It will just be a constant reminder. It's not meant to be a reminder of the junk you've been through or the pain we've endured, but a reminder of the victory that Jesus has given you. Scars become the evidence that you are healed from your wounds.

Your scars will tell your story. It may take a while to heal, but when they finally do, you will be restored. Your scars are a picture of His glory in your life, and as you show off your marks of victory you can give glory to His indescribable grace.

How do your wounds affect you today? Where do you see them manifesting themselves in the current way you think and act? What would it look like if Jesus healed these parts in your life in a perfect world? How do they affect your current relationships?

Grave Clothes

> "When he had said this, Jesus called in a loud voice, 'Lazarus, come out!' The dead man came out, his hands and feet wrapped with strips of linen, and a cloth around his face. Jesus said to them, 'Take off the grave clothes and let him go.'"
>
> **John 11:43-44**

Go back into scripture and read the whole story of Lazarus from the beginning of chapter 11. We see the vast authority that Jesus had to heal in these moments. When Martha and Mary thought all was lost, and Lazarus had passed his time to be healed, that's when Jesus came in and worked a huge miracle. We can absorb a lot of truth from this passage about healing, but we need to also consider a different perspective of this story.

Lazarus was dead. Jesus brought him back to life. When Lazarus exited the tomb, one of Jesus' first commands was to take off his grave clothes. This makes a lot of sense right? The cloth and linen probably stunk a little bit from being around a man who was dead for *four* days, it was probably constricting and uncomfortable for him. Ultimately, it was the wrappings for a *dead* man! Why in the world would he want to stay in grave clothes when he is clearly alive?

This is seemingly a logical conclusion, and yet how many of us walk around in our "grave clothes?" We have redemption, healing, peace, wholeness and life given to us when we believe in the name of Jesus Christ, and yet we walk around as though we are still dead! We live out of this "dead" mentality, as if we haven't received the greatest gift in the world- righteousness and wholeness.

Jesus desires so passionately to do a miracle in your life. He rose from the dead, and He wants to raise you too. He wants to raise your marriage from the dead, your relationships from the dead, your self-esteem from the dead, and the list goes on! He wants to give you an abundant and lavish life. In fact, when you accept Christ, that life is already living in you! Now you have to take heart in that truth, take off your grave clothes and walk out this new life you've been granted!

Reflect on your notes from this week and consider the things in your life that have kept you from walking in abundant and free life. Pray and meditate on God's truth: that He longs for you to walk in a new life of wholeness. Listen to His voice tonight; what is He speaking to you about?

_____

_____

_____

_____

_____

_____

_____

_____

_____

_____

_____

_____

_____

_____

_____

_____

_____

_____

Magnify

"A large crowd followed and pressed around him. And a woman was there who had been subject to bleeding for twelve years. She had suffered a great deal under the care of many doctors and had spent all she had, yet instead of getting better she grew worse. When she heard about Jesus, she came up behind him in the crowd and touched his cloak, because she thought, 'If I just touch his clothes, I will be healed.' Immediately her bleeding stopped and she felt in her body that she was freed from her suffering."

Mark 5:24b-29

Yesterday we read about Lazarus being raised from the dead. We saw the prime example of how God can do miracles in our lives at any moment of our journey. But there are still times when we feel as though we are too far gone, as if our wound is too deep and has been there for far too long.

The Gospel of Mark tells this story about a woman who had been bearing a heavy burden for twelve years. Twelve years she suffered with an illness! You can imagine her journey of struggle- after twelve years of suffering her problem was probably so big that it consumed her entire identity. She was so lost in what she suffered from that she was even known for her illness, not her name, not who she was, but what her problem was.

Have you ever felt like this? That your brokenness consumed your entire identity? That you lost sight of who you really are because all you could see was the giant problem taking up your entire view? Sometimes we feel so defeated, so weighted down by our problems, that we lose sight of God's promises. We begin to focus more on how we are broken rather than how God can heal us.

The road to recovery starts with a perspective shift. We have to start magnifying God's truth in our life rather that Satan's lie. As we start seeing the majesty of who God is and what He desires to do in our life, we begin to refocus who we truly are. Our problems don't look so big, so consuming, or so large over our life, because we see in the greater picture what God wants to do through that problem. God wants to heal our brokenness, and take ourselves out of our cemented mess, because that's simply not who we are.

In the process of us becoming whole, we must consider not just what we have done and has been done to us, but how we look at ourselves. Our perception of ourselves and what we magnify in our lives will dictate how we live. How do you describe yourself and how do you define yourself? Now who does God say you are? (Look in scripture to define what God thinks.)

_____

_____

_____

_____

_____

_____

_____

_____

_____

_____

_____

_____

_____

_____

_____

_____

_____

_____

I've grown up in a loving Christian family and have always been taught God's word. I always attended Sunday school, youth groups, and felt I was a good girl following after Christ, but I never had a real relationship with God. Throughout my life I've struggled with my physical image. Growing up I was the girl with glasses, no makeup, and a ponytail hairstyle. Not to mention, I was always overweight for my age. When high school came along I discovered makeup and boys....surprise, surprise for a teenage girl. At that point I began to play sports, lost some weight, and started to gain confidence in myself. Shortly after, I was introduced to a circle of friends who thought it was cool to party and drink and talk to boys, lots of boys. I liked the idea of being paid attention to, so I was quick to involve myself in the things my friends did in order to gain approval. However, deep down I longed not only for someone to give me a compliment or have a conversation with me, but I longed to be loved, cared for, and appreciated for the love I have to give in return.

All throughout college I continued a sinful lifestyle, seeking attention in whatever way possible. Most of the time I would try to gain attention by drinking in hopes that I would find someone who would want to love me. For years I struggled with keeping one foot in the church and the other in the ways of the world, resulting in what most would call a "lukewarm Christian." Numerous times God tried to stop me in my tracks and call me back to Him because He knew my behaviors would only hurt me in the end, leaving me empty and even more unloved than before. God had me marked as His child from the very beginning of my life, but I was choosing my own path. I didn't listen to God. I thought I could find fulfillment and love on my own, so I continued to seek attention through hopeless relationships.

It wasn't until my most recent relationship that I realized I needed God more than anything. Growing up I had always dreamed of marrying a Christian man, someone who would seek God with me and would someday want to raise a family in the church. But, my lifestyle drew me to non-believers over and over again, until I met the most recent man I dated. We went to the same church, the same college, we did everything together, and soon fell in love. This man loved me like I always wanted to be loved. He told me I was beautiful, he valued me, he wanted to see me succeed, and he helped me out of my sinful lifestyle that I so desperately wanted to leave behind. I thought it was so wonderful to be dating someone who professed to be a Christian like I did! I thought to myself, God finally gave me a man in my life that would take me out of my sin and pull me closer to God. We made all kinds of future plans together to get married and have a family. But soon our love for each other was placed above our love for God. We idolized each other like gods, and our own relationships and walks with the one true God suffered greatly. I knew I wasn't in the right place with God but I wasn't ready to make any drastic moves to change this. I was comfortable and happy in my relationship with this man as it had fulfilled so many of my desires and dreams.

But God had a different plan for my life and removed the man that I loved so much so that I could find true love in Him. God had separated us so that we could seek Him on our own, whole-heartedly, without any distractions. Those first weeks after our breakup I felt like my whole world just shattered and there was nothing I could do about it. I felt such extreme brokenness, hurt, and pain that I would find myself doing nothing but crying on my bed praying that God would bring us back together. At that moment I couldn't see why God wanted us to be apart. All I could see was the immense pain my heart felt to be separated from the one I love. I felt like I lost everything I had planned for my future. I felt like life was sucked right out of me.

What I couldn't see in that moment was that God was pulling me into the wilderness so that He could get me alone to speak to me, comfort me, love me unconditionally, and be the refuge that He is! I had always heard that people in trying times surrendered their lives to Christ, so I too chose to surrender my entire life to God, trusting that He would bring me through the loneliness and hurt that I felt. I began to read the Bible every day and journaled my prayers to God knowing that God saw what I was going through and would be by my side in every step. He planned these events to happen because He loves me and He wants to be the first love of my life. He wants to be all of my life.

A few days after that breakup I decided to go to Vintage, a local college ministry. Vintage was a familiar place to me but I had fallen away from it through college. That night I went alone, trusting that God brought me to this lonely, broken place in my life for a purpose. I had expectation that He would show up and show me something. And He did! That night at Vintage He put two awesome girls in my path who I had not met before. Christ had used them that night to introduce to me some amazing Christian girls who would mentor me in my walk with God and show me what a godly woman should look like. God gave me these women to encourage me and help me grow with Him, providing exactly what I needed at that moment.

Tracy

Weekly Reflection

Take a few moments to quiet yourself before the Lord. Find your comfy spot, or retreat to a place where you often meet with the Lord. In that place, allow your heart, mind and soul to rest into the presence of God. Turn off the distractions, put your to-do list away, and simply be in the present moment. This is your time to be transparent with the Lord, to lay before him your wounds, hurts and struggles, and lift up your requests and deepest desires. You may praise Him, sit in the stillness and listen, or cry to release pain or hurt. The only thing you need to be is real with your heavenly Papa. You may pray the prayer below, or dive into your own. May this time be a blessing to your heart; may the Lord speak to you in new ways; may you allow the comforting and healing hands of our Father reach out to you; and may you allow the peace and joy of the Holy Spirit to pour over you.

Lord Jesus,

I am expecting to hear your voice tonight. Open my heart and my mind to experience and hear your truth in a new way. I lay my wounds and brokenness before you in hope and anticipation that you will heal it all. May I hear new revelation tonight. May I see you and your truth in a new light. Wrap your grace around me and speak softly to your daughter. I am here to listen.

Amen.

Dear Jesus,

_____

_____

_____

_____

_____

_____

Stand

> "He took her by the hand and said to her, 'Talitha koum!' (which means 'Little girl, I say to you, get up!')."
>
> **Mark 5:41**

Read the entire story of this little girl in Mark 5:21-43. It piggy backs off the story of the woman who was sick for twelve years. There was a time in my life when I was drowning in my brokenness. There was a period of time when I literally found myself crying on my bedroom floor, just praying to have hope- hope that there was a better tomorrow, hope that there was a blessing on its way, hope that my life could be redeemed.

As I cried out to God, I wish I could say there was moment of tremendous healing when everything got better. I wish that I could give you a miraculous story about how God instantaneously made my pain go away and my depression dissolved. But I can't, because that didn't happen.

What I can say is that the journey of healing has been long. It's been tough and vigorous. It's been full of exhausting battles. I can also say that in the battlefield of my mind and my heart I have had some breathtaking victories- victories that I never dreamed I could have.

All of those battles started with one step, a single moment when I decided to move forward. Jesus told the dead girl, "Talitha koum," which means, "Little girl, get up!" I think that this is where redemption starts- with simply standing up, with making the choice that we aren't going to live our lives cemented in our junk, and with finally saying that we are going to walk the road with Jesus to freedom and restoration!

What does your first step look like? Is it getting a mentor or accountability person? Is it simply believing that God Has a better tomorrow for you? Or is it maybe obeying a command that God has been laying on your heart for a while?

_____

_____

_____

_____

_____

_____

_____

_____

_____

_____

_____

_____

_____

_____

_____

_____

Saints

> "But you are a chosen people, a royal priesthood, a holy nation,
> God's special possession, that you may declare the praises of him who
> called you out of darkness into his wonderful light."
>
> **1 Peter 2:9**

W
e have talked a lot about our identity in this study. We have learned that we are holy in the sight of God. We are blameless before Him. We are clothed in His righteousness and we are heirs to His throne. We have talked about the importance of us preaching to ourselves this message of who we are, and we have literally laid out a sermon for ourselves to remind us who we belong to. We have also asked ourselves the question of how we think of ourselves. What lens do we see ourselves through and how do we actually define ourselves?

Do you know why we focus on this so much? Because we can never walk in true freedom until we know who we truly are, who we truly belong to, and the magnificence of what God wants us to be.

Just like God pinpointed the nation of Israel, and just like He descended from His heavenly throne and literally hand-picked the Israelites out of slavery, He is doing the same thing to you. He has called you out from His heavenly throne, looking straight at you and released you from your shackles to bring you into freedom.

More than just freedom, He has declared you a saint. A saint, literally meaning "holy one." We learned what the definition of holy was in week one; it means being set apart, and separate from everything else because it is sacred. You are set apart, you are distinct, you are a saint in Christ, and a holy woman of God.

So what does that mean for you? It's great to just call yourself a saint, but what depth of practicality does it have? It means that God has bigger plans for your life than you can imagine. It means that you are not just another person with another ho-hum life. You are chosen by God to be completely healed from your brokenness. You are chosen by God to bring His heavenly kingdom to this world.

Is it difficult to believe that you are handpicked by God and that you are a saint through Christ? Where are you at in the process of seeing your identity in a new perspective? What is God saying to you about who you are and what God is calling you to for His Kingdom?

Seeds

"Praise be to the God and Father of our Lord Jesus Christ,
who has blessed us in the heavenly realms with every spiritual
blessing in Christ."

Ephesians 1:3

I feel like as Christians we have a fallback prayer when we run out of things to pray for. Or not even when we run out of things to say, but when we just naturally fall into the same pattern of prayer. I have definitely caught myself doing it plenty of times! "Lord bless me. Bless this person. Bless Penny Sue. Bless Penny Sue's dog," etc. Now I'm not saying this is a bad thing to pray! Heck, Jabez in 1 Chronicles prayed that he would be blessed indeed and the Lord granted him his request.

But, I don't think we all fully grasp how much we've already been blessed. Not even in a monetary sense, but in a spiritual sense. Ephesians tells us that we have every spiritual blessing placed within us when we are saved. The moment that you bring Christ into your life, you are equipped! Imparted upon you is positively everything you will ever need to walk you through this life and *every* thing you need to become who God wants you to be.

However, you don't always see the fullness of those blessings right away. All of the imparted grace, truth, strength, joy, patience, and wisdom are rooted in you, but it just hasn't borne any fruit yet! When you plant the seed of a beautiful flower, you don't place it in the ground, cover it in dirt, and then instantaneously expect the flower to bloom. But you know that everything that is required to make that beautiful flower grow is in that tiny seed.

You have everything you need within you to be the woman that God wants you to be and to do everything that God wants you to do. You have every piece of joy, every ounce of strength, and every speck of self-control you need to evolve into the woman God knows you can be. So instead of praying for more blessings, pray that you see how you are already blessed, and that God would use what is already in you to walk out what He calls you to do.

What blessings need to come into full bloom in your life? Are you needing patience, strength, hope, love, kindness? Look at Galatians 5:22-23. What blessings do you need to help you overcome what you are enduring right now? Write out a prayer asking God for it.

_____

_____

_____

_____

_____

_____

_____

_____

_____

_____

_____

_____

_____

_____

_____

_____

_____

Perfect Love

> "This is how love is made complete among us so that we will have confidence on the day of judgment: In this word we are like Jesus. There is no fear in love. But perfect love drives out fear, because fear has to do with punishment. The one who fears is not made perfect in love"
>
> **1 John 4: 17-18**

P erfect love: It's hard, no, impossible, to imagine what that looks and feels like. For us in a broken, sin filled world, we can't even fathom what perfect, unconditional love is like. And because we can't wrap our minds around untainted love, we can't fully understand God's love. Or further, we can't fully understand God Himself, because He is love!

God is love. God is in you. Therefore you have God's love within you! When we often think about love, we think about flowery feelings, moonlight walks on the beach and butterflies in our tummy. But God's love breaks that definition apart, and blows us away with what His love can do.

His love that resides in us does two things, among many more. God's love casts out all fear. All fear. God declares that He is control of everything; He will take care of us, protect us and provide for us. When we place our trust in that firm foundation, we literally don't have anything to be afraid of! God's got it all in His hands; He will fight for us and give us victory. Therefore we no longer have to be afraid!

His love also casts out all condemnation. We know Romans 8:1 says, "There is now no condemnation for those who are in Christ Jesus." That was something the law could never do; the law could only wipe away external sin, but not clear a guilt-ridden conscience. The Spirit of God within us clears us of all shame, guilt and condemnation for our sin and mistakes. As Hebrews 9:14 says, "The blood of Jesus cleanses our conscience!"

Many of us still hold onto our guilt and fear. We live out in that mess. But God says, "I am love, I am in you, therefore you are filled with my perfect love. You have nothing to fear and nothing to be ashamed of. You are made perfect in my love."

What sins or mistakes are you still harboring guilt for? What fears are you still holding on to for dear life? Why haven't you been able to let those things go, and how does this impact how you have been seeing your identity in Christ? Ask Jesus to start weeding out those fears and feelings of guilt and condemnation.

_____

_____

_____

_____

_____

_____

_____

_____

_____

_____

_____

_____

_____

_____

_____

_____

_____

_____

Triggers

> "Therefore let us stop passing judgment on one another.
> Instead, make up your mind not to put any stumbling block or obstacle
> in the way of a brother or sister."
>
> **Romans 14:13**

We all have triggers. You know those things that just make your blood boil? Those things that as soon as you detect them in your presence they push a button which sets into motion a spring-loaded emotional response?

Growing up I was the chubby girl. The girl who rocked braces, glasses and a glorious uni-brow all throughout middle school. I was a superb sight! While the Lord had changed me physically over the years, deep down inside I still felt like that boyish, awkward little girl. So as I was in the process of uprooting that disgusting lie, it was crucial for me to be sensitive to what things went into my mind and in front of my eyes. While waiting in the check-out line, I used to flip through the magazines with perfectly airbrushed women, and of course I would immediately feel like junk about myself. So what did I do? I stopped looking at those magazines! It was a trigger in my life that simply sparked an entire emotional and mental tailspin of lies.

In Romans 14:13, I wish that Paul would have added "ourselves," to the end of "brother or sister." We need to be conscious of what things in our lives are stumbling blocks for us. We have to be sensitive to the areas that God is working on in us, and determine what things in our lives add to our emotional imbalance or feed the lies that are being rooted out.

Sometimes you will have triggers that you can only weed out for a season of life, like maybe contact with a specific friend or family member. Others may need to get the permanent cut. You don't need to make the healing process any more difficult than it has to be, so if you can rid your life of unnecessary battles, do it!

Looking to yesterday's response, what things are being worked on in you by God? What triggers are presently in your life that God is calling you to be sensitive to and root out?

_____

_____

_____

_____

_____

_____

_____

_____

_____

_____

_____

_____

_____

_____

_____

_____

_____

_____

_____

G race... what is grace? Grace is a gift from God to his people to save them through his son Jesus Christ. Everyone is presented with this gift; it's our choice whether or not we receive it. When we do receive this amazing gift our lives change and our relationship with God becomes a beautiful story. There is always a beginning of a story, in this case it's our grace story, and this is mine.

I grew up in a very non-Christian home. Alcohol and drugs were a very big burden on my family. Two parents not married and my dad mostly lived out-of-state for jobs. I spent every single day at my best friend's house and it's through them that I was able to hear about Jesus for the first time. I got involved with Vacation Bible School and church every Sunday. I had no idea what I was listening to, all I knew is that I was hanging out with my friends. As I got older my family life got worse, but my knowledge for Christ got bigger. I was going to youth events and was attending two youth groups. I was on the leader board for one of them. It seemed that the harder things got at home the more I plugged myself into the church. One of the amazing things about God is that He has His owns plans for us. Even though I may not have been purposely listening, He still got a hold of my attention. I was baptized at a Christian youth conference in 2001. This was one of the most amazing days of my life. Through the years my relationship with God was all over the place. There would be times where I dedicate my life and serve Him with my whole heart. I was blessed to go on some mission trips; Costa Rica and New Orleans for hurricane Katrina. But then there were times where I was on the total other end of the spectrum. I had my first relationship with a guy. I lost my virginity to him and I did things that I'm not proud of. I lived like that for a year of my life, a year of my life where my eyes were not turned on God. But all I could think was that I didn't need God or my family. This guy loved me and he looked at me like I was the greatest thing that had ever happen to him. Well that didn't last long, apparently he looked at a lot of girls that way. This was a really bad period in my life. My boyfriend cheated on me with his ex and she thought she was pregnant. My dad was living with some other woman and playing daddy to her daughter. The worst was my mom: her drinking was killing her. There were many times that I woke up to her having seizures, so intoxicated that I found her laying naked in the bathroom screaming that she just wanted to kill herself. I remember weeping in my bedroom asking God why had he left me? Why? I know I was not on the right track, but did I really deserve this? I felt His arms wrap around me and whisper tenderly in my ear "I have not and will never leave or forsake you." He showed me of all the examples He was there for me, I just wasn't looking. Once I started a "real" relationship with God that's when He started to bless me. I met who is now my husband and my best friend. We are both in a relationship with Christ, but that doesn't mean that we don't mess up. We have bumps and bruises, and even gashes. As long as we keep going back God He is faithful, He has proven that in more ways than one even when we don't deserve it.

One thing that I have come to learn is that God's gift of grace doesn't just happen once. It is an everyday thing that we need to choose to accept.

Kimberly

Weekly Reflection

Take a few moments to quiet yourself before the Lord. Find your comfy spot, or retreat to a place where you often meet with the Lord. In that place, allow your heart, mind and soul to rest into the presence of God. Turn off the distractions, put your to-do list away, and simply be in the present moment. This is your time to be transparent with the Lord, to lay before him your wounds, hurts and struggles, and lift up your requests and deepest desires. You may praise Him, sit in the stillness and listen, or cry to release pain or hurt. The only thing you need to be is real with your heavenly Papa. You may pray the prayer below, or dive into your own. May this time be a blessing to your heart; may the Lord speak to you in new ways; may you allow the comforting and healing hands of our Father reach out to you; and may you allow the peace and joy of the Holy Spirit to pour over you.

Lord Jesus,

I am expecting to hear your voice in this moment. Open my heart and my mind to experience and hear your truth in a new way. I lay my wounds and brokenness before you, in hope and anticipation that you will heal it all. May I hear new revelation this week! May I see you and your truth in a new light! Wrap your grace around me and speak softly to your daughter. I am here to listen.

Amen.

Dear Jesus,

_____

_____

_____

_____

_____

_____

If I Can

> "Jesus asked the boy's father, 'How long has he been like this?' 'From childhood,' he answered. 'It has often thrown him into fire or water to kill him. But if you can do anything take pity on us and help us.' 'If you can'?' said Jesus. 'Everything is possible for one who believes.'"
>
> **Mark 9:21-23**

It's time for another heart check. At this point we have truly dug down deep into the incredible power of God's Spirit and love. We have explored what God truly desires to do in us and the work that He wants to do with our lives.

But at this point, we have to reexamine our heart. I think it is natural for us to read this sort of devotional, and see truths, and say that we believe them. We may hear these things all the time, and so they become part of our conscience. But, applying it to our life is something completely different. It's great to know these truths in theory, but practicing them daily is another thing entirely.

We reach a point like the father of the boy in Mark 9:21-23. He knew who Jesus was and what He was capable of. Yet, when he asked Jesus to heal his son, he added on to his request, "if you can."

I think that's where a lot of us camp. We believe who Jesus is and what He is capable of doing, but we tack on the extra "if you can." We still doubt that God can or would actually work a miracle in our life! We ask God to heal our hearts, to rid us of guilt and fear, to bind up our wounds, but we unnecessarily add on, "if you can, Jesus."

What does Jesus say? "Everything is possible for one who believes!" Anything is possible when you believe. When you place your faith and trust in the one who holds every one of your wounds- every shattered piece of your heart in His hands- you can live with confidence that He will show you what He is capable of. And He is truly capable of anything!

Do you still add an "if you can" when you ask Jesus to heal you? What things are keeping you from trusting fully? Do you doubt that God can really redeem you? If so, pray that He would reveal Himself to you in miraculous ways.

_____

_____

_____

_____

_____

_____

_____

_____

_____

_____

_____

_____

_____

_____

_____

_____

_____

_____

Fragrance

> "When they saw the courage of Peter and John and realized that they
> were unschooled, ordinary men, they were astonished and they took
> note that these men had been with Jesus."
>
> **Acts 4:13**

Grace gives us one of the greatest gifts we can ever receive. It allows us to once more be in the presence of our God. Through Jesus' blood, God can now dwell within us at every moment of the day. When that grace pours over our life, we experience God in a whole new way because we now have Him dwelling in us.

We can understand the presence of God in our lives just like being close with someone wearing a powerful perfume. We find that when we hang out with her all day, we get home and realize that we smell like them too! This same idea flows into our relationship with Jesus. When we become aware of His ever-present nature in our life, His sweet fragrance will start to rub off on us! His majesty, His love, his peace, His nature, His patience, His compassion- it will all start to manifest in our lives!

The presence of God also grants us favor in every moment of our life. Because He is always with us, we can tap into His supernatural wisdom, His unconditional love, and His surpassing knowledge. When we let the Spirit flow in us, amazing things start happening! His presence will guide us, direct us, and refine us as we start to listen to His divine whisper in us.

The power behind both of these blessings is that you have to be aware of God's presence in order for you to start experiencing the results. You have to take part in the constant whisper conversation between yourself and God at each moment of the day; make Jesus the continual force that enters into your every moment! I'm not saying you should just sit in your bedroom in a quiet time all day in formal prayer. Practicing the presence of God is about making a decision to pray throughout the day, about the tiniest and biggest things. It's about being aware of Jesus being with you at every moment of the day, ready and being ready for the blessings that are already in you to continue flowing out!

Think about the last week, how aware have you been of God's presence in your day to day routine? Make a commitment to attempt to be in a divine whisper with God regularly throughout the day. On Monday of next week come back here and write down your experience.

_____

_____

_____

_____

_____

_____

_____

_____

Return here next Monday to reflect on your encounters!

_____

_____

_____

_____

_____

_____

_____

_____

Peace

> "Let your gentleness be evident to all. The Lord is near. Do not be anxious about anything, but in every situation, by prayer and petition, with thanksgiving, present your requests to God. And the peace of God, which transcends all understanding, will guard your hearts and your minds in Christ Jesus."
> **Philippians 4:5-7**

Anxiety is a real issue that plagues a majority of people. We are pressed from stress, work, family responsibilities, horrible news reports, lack of finances, and the list could go on! We feel the burden of high strung, unceasing amounts of stress that fly at us continually all throughout our week.

Peace and rest from God amongst all of those things seems nearly unobtainable. How can we experience peace when our checking account is in the negative, our family is falling apart, or we have a zillion deadlines for work? How can we rest when money needs to be made, our kids have soccer practice, and we feel that we need to be super woman to the entire world?

Just as we need to practice the presence of Jesus in our life, we also have to practice a spirit of peace through the Holy Spirit. God grants us peace in every situation we are in. Why? Because He is taking care of us; no problem is too big or too small for Him! He is a God who loves to show us His miraculous wonders! So as we keep Him as the focus of our mind, every worry or anxious thought can be set against the faithful promises of God.

However, it is essential that you take part in this peace. God calls you to rest, and in order to obey this, you must set time aside for Him to rejuvenate you. If you feel like you haven't had a time for just you and Jesus in a while, then it's time for a date! I have even heard of people having dinner with Jesus, just sitting, eating, and talking with their Savior. What an incredible dinner conversation that probably is!

God gives us a peace that surpasses all of our circumstances and life situations. He will give us rest from the chaos of the world when we allow His Spirit and promises to invade every arena of our life. Allow yourself the margin in your life to take part in His promised rest and peace.

Read Matthew 11:28. What things in your life are making you weary? Now how do those anxious thoughts fail in comparison to God's promises to us? Ask God to give you scripture to meditate on when these worries enter your mind.

_____

_____

_____

_____

_____

_____

_____

_____

_____

_____

_____

_____

_____

_____

_____

_____

_____

Protection

> "And having disarmed the powers and authorities, he made a public spectacle of them, triumphing over them by the cross."
>
> **Colossians 2:15**

In the Old Testament, we see God's protective hand shielding the nation of Israel against their enemies. We read stories about how God gave victory to the Israelites and literally wiped out each one of their opponents. We see that example of God's protection, and then we compare it to our lives today. We feel as if we don't "hear" God as they did in the Old Testament, or we don't "see" God tangibly showing His protective powers today. But we are protected so much more fully than people were in the Old Testament. God's hand of security has not ceased-it has just manifested itself in new ways.

Each and every day we face two forces of opposition. We experience the intense battles between things that we can see and things that we can't see; between the physical and spiritual realms of life. So, while we endure environmental and relational pressures, we are simultaneously being bombarded with attacks from Satan in our hearts and minds.

Through grace, Christ has been able to take His place within us, not just to protect us from the outward battles but the inward as well. While we may not see God's hand swooping down plucking us up out of terrible circumstances, we can know that He is working to keep us from harm in ways that we aren't even aware of.

As we discuss this journey of healing, of turning wounds into scars, we have to pay special attention to our covering in the mental and spiritual battles throughout our day. As you begin to step out to conquer your fears and doubts and make yourself vulnerable to God's restoring hand, you will, without a shadow of a doubt, face more spiritual battles. Satan does not want you walking out the promises of God, and He will bring out all his weapons to keep you in your cement! You must walk firm in the truth, knowing that He who is in you is greater than he who is in the world. Take heart, knowing that God is your covering, shield, security, and armor against every attack you encounter.

Read Ephesians 6:10-18. Meditate on this passage with the knowledge that you already have victory in every battle through Christ. List here the attacks with which Satan comes against you; what lies does He repeatedly whisper? Even more, list the truths from God that combat those lies.

_____

_____

_____

_____

_____

_____

_____

_____

_____

_____

_____

_____

_____

_____

_____

_____

_____

Provision

> "Then he [Jesus] took the seven loaves and the fish, and when he had given thanks, he broke them and gave them to the disciples, and they in turn to the people. They all ate and were satisfied. Afterward the disciples picked up seven basketfuls of broken pieces that were left over."
>
> **Matthew 15:36-37**

Provision is a tricky topic for people to talk about. It is such a tangible part of life, and such a sticky subject when it comes to faith, especially for people who struggle with financial matters- the single mom who is working three jobs and still can't make it, the woman whose husband was laid off while having three children to raise, the college student who has no extra time in the midst of their studies to take on another part time job. No matter what circumstances we are in, finances are a pressure point for many of us.

I personally have seen the ample provision of God. Recently I have been in an extremely tight financial bind. Jobs have been inconsistent and extra time between school and ministry have disallowed me from holding a full time position. But somehow God has provided for my every need. I look at my bank account and somehow it seems as if there is more there than I expected. Random jobs and sources of income pop up at exactly the right moment. I have experienced the blessings of "fishes and loaves" as described here in Matthew.

As a child of God, and an heir to God's throne, God promises to keep you close and take care of you, His prized possession. He will not leave you or forsake you, even in the most practical of ways. As you are obedient in doing what He calls you to do, and as you are diligent in being faithful to what He has given you, He will bless that generous and honorable heart! He says to you that as you give your time, money, and heart to Him and His people, He will bless you in ways you can't imagine and will provide for you as you serve others.

I know this is a hard concept to understand. It's a difficult truth to believe in our hearts and minds. But take a chance and challenge God on this matter; see if He doesn't blow your mind with what He can do!

Read through Malachi 3:10 and Luke 6:38. Are you struggling to trust God in the tangible provision in your life? Write out a prayer surrendering these areas of your life and expect Him to show you what He can do.

I've known Christ since I was a little girl, well, "known." I went to church on Sundays, checked it off the to-do list and went about the rest of my week thinking that because I went to church and was a good person, I was a Christian. I went off to college and lived life how I wanted; one foot in the world with one foot caught in my Christian background, knowing I was sinning but using that good person principle to quiet my conscience. That only lasts for so long, especially when you can't figure out for the life of you why you're so unhappy and unfulfilled inside. But you put a smile on your face and act like everything is fine. One day when you graduate, when you have a great job, when you find the man of your dreams and have a big house and the perfect life, you'll be happy. Right?

In the summer of 2010 I was in Chicago, getting ready to graduate Chiropractic school and trying to piece together that life I thought I was supposed to build for myself. That was when God stepped in, He had let me do things my way for awhile but now it was time to do things His way. My boyfriend at the time ended our relationship, I couldn't find a job, and 2 weeks before I was set to graduate, I found out I was going to have nowhere to live and no family to lean on in Chicago. Piece by piece, God removed from my life all of the things I was desperately clinging to, things that would keep me in the life I wanted, things that I thought would make me happy. He gave me one choice and one choice only: go home and seek Him. So home I went; I was bitter, confused, depressed, completely and utterly broken. It's a lonely and awful place to be angry with God. Slowly over the next 8 months God softened my heart and as I found myself in a routine, forming a life again, He was working in ways I couldn't imagine. Finally on April 3, 2011, a preacher was teaching a sermon entitled "The Next Fifty in WNY" and he was in Jeremiah 29:4-7, Israel's exile in Babylon. I felt God speaking directly to me that morning. That was the day my life changed and God had my full attention. That was the day I stopped resisting what He was trying to do in me. I had a long way to go, a lot to learn, and things didn't happen overnight but the difference was that no longer was it about me and what I wanted! It was about what God's best was for me and letting Him accomplish it! I let Him be my anchor, my source of strength, joy and completeness. I made the decision once and for all to live my life for God and God alone. In the past I had only seen this in shades of gray but I realized how wrong I had been. It was black and white and I needed to make a choice. I chose God and my life has never been the same because His plan was so much better than mine. It is a beautiful and peaceful place to be in love with God.

Sasha

Weekly Reflection

Take a few moments to quiet yourself before the Lord. Find your comfy spot, or retreat to a place where you often meet with the Lord. In that place, allow your heart, mind and soul to rest into the presence of God. Turn off the distractions, put your to-do list away, and simply be in the present moment. This is your time to be transparent with the Lord, to lay before him your wounds, hurts and struggles, and lift up your requests and deepest desires. You may praise Him, sit in the stillness and listen, or cry to release pain or hurt. The only thing you need to be is real with your heavenly Papa. You may pray the prayer below, or dive into your own. May this time be a blessing to your heart; may the Lord speak to you in new ways; may you allow the comforting and healing hands of our Father reach out to you; and may you allow the peace and joy of the Holy Spirit to pour over you.

Lord Jesus,

I am expecting to hear your voice in this moment. Open my heart and my mind to experience and hear your truth in a new way. I lay my wounds and brokenness before you, in hope and anticipation that you will heal it all. May I hear new revelation this week! May I see you and your truth in a new light! Wrap your grace around me and speak softly to your daughter. I am here to listen.

Amen.

Dear Jesus,

_____

_____

_____

_____

_____

_____

Remember to go back to Day 3 of last week, "Fragrance,"
to reflect on your divine whispers with God.

One Name

> "Then Peter said, 'Silver or gold I do not have, but what I do have I give
> you. In the name of Jesus Christ of Nazareth, walk.' Taking him
> by the right hand, he helped him up, and instantly the man's feet
> and ankles became strong."
>
> **Acts 3:6-7**

One name gave sight to the blind. One name made the crippled walk. One name cast out demons. One name multiplied a handful of fish and loaves into a banquet that fed thousands. One name calmed a raging sea. One single command from one name would change a person's life forever. One name sacrificed his life for yours.

That one name isn't yours- that one name is Jesus. We tend to put pressure on ourselves to heal ourselves, provide for ourselves, and take care of ourselves and everyone else in our lives! We place the weight of responsibility for everything in this life upon our own shoulders. It is a weight that completely overwhelms us because it is a weight that only Jesus can bear!

In the same instance that we put the pressure of the world on ourselves, we feel guilty for the things that we can't accomplish. Satan tricks us into thinking that life is all about us. It's about the all the things we have to do, all the things we are incapable of doing, and all the things that we did that we shouldn't have done! Satan wants us to believe that the world is centered around, run by, and dependent on us! (And that we are failing at this!)

But it's not, and we are not. The one name that has all power and all authority is not our own; it's Jesus's. But the most glorious part about grace is that Jesus is within us. His authority, His power, His healing, His freedom, His love- they are all within us.

Take a deep breath and allow God to take the throne in your life. Allow Jesus to be the one name that heals all, controls all, provides all and protects all.

What areas in your life have you tried to control and tried to play God? What areas is the Lord calling you to surrender to allow Him to be God?

_____

_____

_____

_____

_____

_____

_____

_____

_____

_____

_____

_____

_____

_____

_____

_____

_____

_____

_____

_____

One Thing

> "She had a sister called Mary, who sat that the Lord's feet listening to what he [Jesus] said. But Martha was distracted by all the preparations that had to be made. She came to him and asked, 'Lord, don't you care that my sister has left me to do the work by myself? Tell her to help me!' 'Martha, Martha,' the Lord answered, 'you are worried and upset about many things, but few things are needed or indeed only one. Mary has chosen what is better, and it will not be taken away from her.'"
>
> **Luke 10: 39-42**

From this passage you find an extremely important question; what is the one thing you need in your life? What is the one thing that, if it falls apart everything else goes haywire? What is the one thing that you need more than anything to make everything else purposeful, full of peace and productive?

We can easily get caught up in the hustle of life. We are easily caught up in trying to be good and do the right things to earn Jesus' approval. We are easily distracted by the worries and anxiety that come with life. We easily drown in the effects of our brokenness, wounds and sin. All of those distractions fight to keep our eyes from our loving King.

Let us imagine the picture of a windshield wiper. We cast our eyes upon the cross, the picture of grace through our windshield. Each lie, each tear of hurt, every piece of sin, every voice of condemnation fights to blur our view. The power and importance of fixing our vision is to be able to see the junk that hinders our view of His love. Sometimes when we fix our eyes on His truth and grace, we only see all the things that fog our vision. If we can see those things through the lens of the cross, we can then push away all the lies with the wiper of His grace. We can toss out every voice of hate. We can throw our sin before our Savior. And then we can see clearly again.

Is Jesus the one thing that you need more than anything else? Is He the lens through which you see every aspect of life? Is He your rest, your comfort, your strength, and your rock? Is your vision set upon Jesus, to the point that everything else is seen through the picture of his grace?

Think about the questions at the end of today's devotional. What is truly your one "thing"? If it isn't Jesus, what have you made it to be?

_____

_____

_____

_____

_____

_____

_____

_____

_____

_____

_____

_____

_____

_____

_____

_____

_____

_____

_____

_____

_____

One Salvation

"For I am not ashamed of the gospel, because it is the power of God
that brings salvation to everyone who believes:
first to the Jew, then to the Gentile."

Romans 1:16

I think I have rededicated my life at least a dozen times. I have been to countless youth camps, church retreats, and Bible studies where the altar call has been given and I felt "called" to respond. The normal routine would commence, where I would go to the front of the church, cry my eyes out in confession for all my sins, and promise Jesus that I would be perfect from then on.

As Christians, we have a tendency to focus primarily on being "saved." We carry around guilt and shame as if it's going out of style because we think that every sin we commit after we are officially "saved" isn't covered. It's as if we have to start the whole "being saved" process all over again because we messed it up the last time!

Salvation comes from the Greek word "soteria" which means "deliverance, preservation, safety and health." Salvation doesn't mean that we are just saved from hell. It isn't a standard to live up to that we have to fulfill in some way. Salvation is belief that God has delivered us from death. He is defending us as His heirs; He is protecting us as His possession and taking care of His children. Salvation is the process of becoming fully restored to God.

Salvation is the journey of us being healed, becoming whole, and being fully redeemed. And that process starts at the moment when we dedicate our life to Christ. But it's a journey that lasts a lifetime, learning to walk in His promises, learning to walk as He does, and learning to trust who He is and what He says He will do.

Have you felt the pressure to continually recommit your life to Christ? How does this view of salvation change how you think about faith?

_____

_____

_____

_____

_____

_____

_____

_____

_____

_____

_____

_____

_____

_____

_____

_____

_____

_____

_____

One Hope

> "Even youths shall faint and be weary, and [selected] young men shall
> feebly stumble and fall exhausted; but those who wait for the Lord
> [who expect, look for, and hope in Him] shall change and renew their
> strength and power; they shall lift their wings and mount up [close to
> God] as eagles [mount up to the sun]; they shall run and not be weary,
> they shall walk and not faint or become tired."
>
> **Isaiah 40:30-31** *(Amplified Version-Classic Edition))*

Being in the waiting room stinks! It smells, it's boring, sometimes it's stressful, and even gross. I think it's in this moment of waiting that our character shines through. We either wait patiently, make the most of our time in those uncomfortable chairs, or we complain, argue, and make the worst of the situation.

Everyone experiences life's waiting rooms. It's often in the midst of those periods of life when the world loses hope. But, we are Jesus' chosen, holy children, set apart and made to be distinct from the rest of the world. When we wait ,we not only don't *lose* hope, but we *gain* it.

That is what separates us from the rest of the world. That is what makes our light shine. That is what keeps us growing and moving. Because while our circumstances may be exactly the same, our reactions can be completely different. It's not about life being easier, but about having a steady hope that gets us through it all.

It seems unnatural to the world that while we wait on the Lord our hope only grows. It seems paradoxical that while we are in the most uncomfortable situations our lives could shine the most.

Your healing process may be long! It may be tiring, and trying too. In fact it will probably be all of those things! But this waiting room is full of work, of persisting and driving full speed ahead. As you live out God's grace and persistently seek after Him, keep your eyes fixed on His glorious hope.

What are you currently waiting for in life? Are you waiting patiently or are you complaining in the process? How can you use this waiting time to bring glory to God?

The One

> "When they kept on questioning him, he straightened up and said to them, 'Let any one of your who is without sin be the first to throw a stone at her.' Again he stooped down and wrote on the ground. At this, those who heard began to go away one at a time, the older ones first, until only Jesus was left, with the woman still standing there. Jesus straightened up and asked her, 'Woman, where are they?' Has no one condemned you?' 'No one, sir,' she said. 'Then neither do I condemn you,' Jesus declared. 'Go now and leave your life of sin.'"
>
> **John 8:7-11**

Read the full story of this woman in John 8:2-11. Can you imagine being this woman? Can you imagine what she was feeling in that moment? Fear probably doesn't even cover what she was experiencing. She knew the law and so she knew that she deserved death. She was living in the juncture between life and death, probably watching her life flash before her eyes.

But then Jesus speaks. And everyone else falls silent. One by one her accusers drop their stone and leave. One by one the judges fall away, and only she and Jesus remain. Can you picture that moment when it's just the woman and Jesus? Can you imagine the beauty of that moment: knowing that every one that could condemn her was gone, and every voice that could place judgment on her had walked away?

We can walk out that moment everyday of our lives. Through grace we are left with just us and Jesus. The voices that tell us we aren't good enough, that we are broken messes, or that we are worthy of being condemned, no longer hold any power. The moment we call on His name He will make sure all those voices are hushed. We are no longer under condemnation, we are no longer deserving death, and we are no longer bound in guilt and shame. The one who has all the authority to condemn us for our sin wipes the slate clean and sets us free!

Let the lies, the voices and the accusers fall away until you are standing alone with Jesus. In that moment, you will be reminded of His mercy and grace, because you are free.

What are your accusers saying to you? Get specific with what the other voices are telling you. Imagine the moment when it's just you and Jesus. What does that look like? How does it make you feel?

_____

_____

_____

_____

_____

_____

_____

_____

_____

_____

_____

_____

_____

_____

_____

_____

_____

_____

I am very blessed because I grew up in a Christian household where God was incredibly important. My mother and father were devout Christians who always stressed the importance of a personal relationship with Christ. We went to church every Sunday, participated in Sunday school, and prayed as a family before every meal and had family devotion time on Sunday evenings. They are far from perfect, but they showed us daily the importance of Christ in their lives.

I am one of four girls. I was the second youngest and struggled to find my place within the family. I was constantly being compared to my older sisters and I wasn't the baby anymore. I felt lost in the shuffle. I got caught up with striving to be perfect because I thought that maybe that would get me noticed. Piano, school, sports, the list goes on and on. The more I tried, the more I failed. I remember being a very angry and frustrated child.

I was eight when I consciously made the decision to accept Jesus Christ as my Lord and Savior at a Billy Graham Crusade. I wanted to have that peace and security in eternity. I saw Jesus as a way to help me with my struggles of perfectionism and my anger issues. I continued to attend Sunday school throughout middle school and high school, growing in my faith. I also was active in church groups as well as volunteering.

After graduation from high school, I went to college at UB. I lived in an apartment with my sister and I started deciding that I didn't like where God was taking me (or hadn't taken me). I decided that I knew better than God and started living life my own way. I let other things and people influence me and get in the way of my relationship with God. This continued for several years. I had dethroned God as the King of my heart and life and placed myself there. Of course time after time my decisions just led to a bigger mess and didn't get me anywhere. I would still occasionally attend church, but I was just attending, I wasn't participating and listening to what God had to tell me. My life was similar to that of the Israelites, a continuous up and down relationship with God. Sin, realize my wrongdoing, and then repent, cycle over and over again.

Years had gone by and my life wasn't any "better." I had finished school but I still didn't have a job, wasn't married, and didn't have kids. I saw myself as a total failure. I was sad and depressed. I was trying to find earthly things to fill the void that I was feeling, but nothing was. I began attending church about three years ago. Through the messages there, I realized that I was never going to find peace and happiness with the world. Only through a personal relationship with Christ and obedience would my life find purpose and meaning. What I had been missing had been there all along and He was just patiently waiting for me. I started to understand that things were never going to get better unless I gave control of my life back over to God. I needed to rediscover and start participating in my relationship with God. Since then, God and I have a constant open dialogue. I spend time in His word and I am learning to quiet my heart so I can hear Him speak to me. He has blessed me beyond what I deserve and has continued to give me an inner peace and realization that the world.

Melissa

Weekly Reflection

Take a few moments to quiet yourself before the Lord. Find your comfy spot, or retreat to a place where you often meet with the Lord. In that place, allow your heart, mind and soul to rest into the presence of God. Turn off the distractions, put your to-do list away, and simply be in the present moment. This is your time to be transparent with the Lord, to lay before him your wounds, hurts and struggles, and lift up your requests and deepest desires. You may praise Him, sit in the stillness and listen, or cry to release pain or hurt. The only thing you need to be is real with your heavenly Papa. You may pray the prayer below, or dive into your own. May this time be a blessing to your heart; may the Lord speak to you in new ways; may you allow the comforting and healing hands of our Father reach out to you; and may you allow the peace and joy of the Holy Spirit to pour over you.

Lord Jesus,

I am expecting to hear your voice in this moment. Open my heart and my mind to experience and hear your truth in a new way. I lay my wounds and brokenness before you, in hope and anticipation that you will heal it all. May I hear new revelation this week! May I see you and your truth in a new light! Wrap your grace around me and speak softly to your daughter. I am here to listen.

Amen.

Dear Jesus,

_____

_____

_____

_____

_____

_____

The Power of Story

> "Then, leaving her water jar, the woman went back to the town and said to the people, 'Come, see a man who told me everything I ever did. Could this be the Messiah?' They came out of the town and made their way toward him."
> "Many of the Samaritans from that town believed in him because of the woman's testimony, "He told me everything I ever did.""
>
> **John 4:28-30 & 39**

We are in the last week of this study. Think over the past twelve weeks. Reflect on everything you have learned. Where are you at with Jesus? Are you in awe of God's goodness and grace? Do you feel stirred to share what God has done *for* you and *in* you?

Read through the whole story of the woman at the well in John 4:1-41. We see an incredible transformation of a woman, all in just a single chapter! What I find most powerful isn't just the story of how she met Jesus, but what flowed from her after she was changed. Verses 39-41 tell about the affects of her metamorphosis.

Jesus impacted her so greatly, He moved her so deeply and loved her so passionately, that she was compelled to tell other people. What she experienced was so powerful that she couldn't contain the joy within her own soul! She had to share her story, she had to explain her experience; and she had to spread the word so others could encounter the man who changed her whole life!

When she opened her mouth and told her story, other lives were changed. Through her testimony she literally changed her town! Your story has just as much power. As you heal, grow and experience Jesus, your story will be molded and crafted as a tool to change this world. But it is a tool that must be used. Jesus calls you to share your story. There are people who are experiencing journeys similar to yours, and you need to breathe encouragement, hope, and life into their story through your own.

Do you feel compelled to tell your story? Have you been so moved that you feel like you have to tell other people about the Jesus that you have experienced? If not, talk to Jesus about it and journal your conversation here.

_____

_____

_____

_____

_____

_____

_____

_____

_____

_____

_____

_____

_____

_____

_____

_____

_____

_____

The Nudge

"Then Jesus came to them and said, 'All authority in heaven and on earth has been given to me. Therefore go and make disciples of all nations, baptizing them in the name of the Father and of the Son and of the Holy Spirit, and teaching them to obey everything I have commanded you. And surely I am with you always, to the very end of the age.'"

Matthew 28:18-20

I love this command from Jesus! We are called to "go" and make disciples of all nations. *All* nations. That means *all* people. Everywhere and anywhere, at every time, and any time.

Everywhere we go we have the opportunity to share Jesus. At any time of the day we can be a vessel of His love. He commands us to share His word, to spread His love and speak His gospel. The gospel is shared through speaking and living. Therefore, we don't have to give a gospel message and lay out the full salvation message to complete strangers. Sometimes we are just expected to love hard and show grace in a world that doesn't know it.

I love to think about these moments as divine appointments. These are preordained opportunities that God has set up for us to be a lamp for other people. But only we can choose if we live out that opportunity or let the moment slip away. God places the divine meeting before us, but we must make the decision to see it and embrace it, or it disappears.

Maybe there is a specific person that you have been feeling nudged to talk to at work or school. Or maybe you have been feeling the nudge to simply love strangers better. Take time throughout the day to ask God to allow you to see these divine appointments and the boldness to embrace them! Your single act of kindness, your moment of sharing love to a stranger, or your sharing your story with a co-worker is all part of the great commission to spread the gospel to all ends of the earth!

What divine appointments have you had recently? Is there someone that has been on your heart to tell your story? How is Jesus speaking to you about fulfilling His commission?

_____

_____

_____

_____

_____

_____

_____

_____

_____

_____

_____

_____

_____

_____

_____

_____

_____

_____

_____

Unfinished

> "However, I consider my life worth nothing to me; my only aim is to finish the race and complete the task the Lord Jesus has given me— the task of testifying to the good news of God's grace."
>
> **Acts 20:24**

We are all a work in progress. We all have things that we are continuing to work on. Each one of us has our things that God is probing, molding, and fixing. Because we live in a broken world, we will always have things that are being refined in our life. We will always be on a journey of being made better, more complete, in wholeness.

I think some of us don't share our stories because we are in the process of transition. We think that because we aren't perfect that we should keep all our imperfections to ourselves. But the process is the point. The story of our healing, the day by day transformation, is the purpose of life. God calls us to share with others what He is doing inside of us. He longs for us to encourage others with what we are enduring.

Eventually each of your wounds *will* become a scar. Those scars will be evidence that your wounds are healed. As you are being made whole, renewed, and mended by the almighty physician, know that your story will impact so many people. And when your wounds are healed, don't be afraid to show the scars!! Share your struggles that you experienced. Express the pain you endured. Allow people to see the scars that were healed by your heavenly Father.

Read over your entries in this devotional. Can you see your story unfold? Each wound, struggle and scar is part of your story that God wants to use for His glory. Looking over your entries, write out your journey of grace with Jesus. What has He shown you about Himself? What has He revealed about you?

_____

_____

_____

_____

_____

_____

_____

_____

_____

_____

_____

_____

_____

_____

_____

_____

_____

_____

_____

An Army

> "So I prophesied as he commanded me, and breath entered them;
> they came to life and stood up on their feet-a vast army."
>
> **Ezekiel 37:10**

Read the whole vision of the valley of the dry bones in Ezekiel 37:1-10. What does your "valley" look like? Are you standing in the midst of a broken family situation? Are you walking through the lives of wounded people at work or school? Or are you simply wandering through a world lost in sin?

We each have our moments as dead soldiers. We each have things in our lives that seem like dry bones without any life in them. But as God's grace flows over our heart and mind, as His Spirit breathes over our brokenness, He is bringing us back to life! And not just to stand alone in the midst of a broken world, but to stand together as others in our life are raised up as well.

I love the last verse of this vision. It places us in the midst of a powerful army, each soldier empowered by the Spirit of God. Each of us is a soldier in the vast army of God.

This world is tainted by sin, mangled by the effects of separation from God, and some people are stuck in the mess of it all. We are charged with the responsibility to stand together, as a vast army to be light to a dark world. Together, as women of God, we unite as one body, under one banner and one Savior. We are all working on our own junk, processing through our own brokenness, and becoming more refined daily.

We each have powerful stories of transformation, of God's hand at work, of God's grace invading our hearts. God has placed those stories within us to impact this world. As we ban together, as women who are doing life together, daily dying to ourselves and letting His love change us, let us charge forward to show the world Jesus' redeeming grace.

What does your valley look like? To whom is God calling you to speak? Who are women with whom you can band together to help you in this journey of life? Pray that the Lord would reveal these things to your heart and that He would surround you with women to encourage, strengthen and empower you!

_____

_____

_____

_____

_____

_____

_____

_____

_____

_____

_____

_____

_____

_____

_____

_____

_____

Greater

> "Very truly I tell you, all who have faith in me will do the works I have
> been doing, and they will do even greater things than these,
> because I am going to the Father."
>
> **John 14:12**

We are often conditioned to expect a mediocre life. To live day in and day out in the monotony of a daily routine. We are trained to believe that we will never get out of our cement. And most of all, we are accustomed to lives that are fueled by guilt and shame with open, unhealed wounds.

But God's grace is bigger. It gives us hope to expect huge things! It moves us so greatly that our lives are completely transformed. Jesus wants us to expect monumental things in this life. He wants us to expect Him to work, expect Him to show up in miraculous ways, and to expect Him to show off all of His incredible, holy glory!

Grace is not just a word that saves us once and leaves us in our mess. Grace is a message that brings total healing. Grace is the promise of God to adopt us as His own. Grace is the spiritual seal declaring that we are absolutely righteous before our heavenly Father. Grace is God at work within us, giving us the strength and desire to obey His word. Grace is God's ultimate gift to His creation. We are the recipients; the ones who He loves unconditionally, pursues relentlessly, and embraces completely.

Grace is the force that allows us to do greater things than even Jesus did. You have that power within you. Accept the gift of grace, believe in the power of His truth, and share His grace with the rest of the world.

What key things has God spoken to you about in this study? Reflect on this process. Write out a prayer for your hopes going forward and expectations for the big things God has planned for you.

I was blessed with a great job, and part of my duties as the family's Nanny was to bring the children to church every Sunday morning. I was not familiar with this church, as I was raised in a small Catholic church. I never understood the true meaning of who God was. After making decisions that were not well thought out, I parted with the family, soon leaving myself and my 20 month old daughter homeless. We ended up in a homeless shelter. At the time, our circumstances were beyond anyone's control who were near to us, such as family or friends. We stayed in the shelter for one month, both experiencing and suffering from severe nightmares nearly causing hospitalization due to the trauma and inability to sleep for days on end. Mandated Bible studies were permitted me to have a Bible nearby. I opened to random pages praying, everyday, hoping something would come through, as far as housing and employment to become stable again. My faith was running thin, and I was coming very close to losing hope. Late in that day on a Friday, I left the shelter. I planned to stay at a former relative's house, and soon move back out-of-state, and leave my hopes for the future behind. The same day that I lost hope, and wanted to give up, I had received a phone call for a job offer that I had interviewed for. I accepted the job, and rethought moving home. Only a few hours later, I had received another phone call, and it was a response to my Craigslist ad for a roommate from a single mother like me. At that point, I knew the Lord was with me, and had answered my prayers in the most amazing way imaginable. By Saturday, I had my daughter and I moved into our new home with an amazing single mother and her infant son. By Monday,

I happily started my new job. I continued going to church, voluntarily on my own, and not as a job duty. I sought the Lord with all my heart. Three months later, I had received a $7,000.00 tax return that I set aside for the rest of the year to stabilize my expenses and never ran into hardship. The Lord had provided me with many other things after that, and continues to bless me in many ways. From that point on, I trusted in God, and built an amazing relationship with Him, and was called to the field I am studying today. If I hadn't gone through that dark time in my life, I would have never had a relationship with the Lord, and not be where I am today.

Mariah

35400519R00099

Made in the USA
Middletown, DE
01 October 2016